# A HouseBeautiful Home Business

### HOW TO START A SUCCESSFUL INTERIORS, HOMEWARES OR FURNITURE BUSINESS

# FROM HOME
# by Emma Jones

An Enterprise Nation book
www.enterprisenation.com

HARRIMAN HOUSE LTD
3A Penns Road
Petersfield
Hampshire
GU32 2EW
GREAT BRITAIN

Tel: +44 (0)1730 233870
Email: enquiries@harriman-house.com
Website: www.harriman-house.com
First published in Great Britain in 2013.
Copyright © Harriman House Ltd

*House Beautiful* is the registered trademark of the National Magazine Company.

ISBN: 9781908003577

British Library Cataloguing in Publication Data
A CIP catalogue record for this book can be obtained from the British Library.

Set in Caslon, Berthold Akzidenz Grotesk and Narziss

# CONTENTS

# ABOUT THE AUTHOR

Emma Jones is a business expert, author and founder of small business community Enterprise Nation. Her books include *Working 5 to 9*, *Go Global: How to take your business to the world* and *Turn Your Talent Into a Business*.

Following a five-year career at an international accounting firm, Emma started her first business at 27. That business was sold 18 months later, and the experience led to Emma's next venture, Enterprise Nation.

Its website (**www.enterprisenation.com**) was launched in 2006 and became the most popular site for home business owners in the UK, attracting over 100,000 visitors each month.

In seven years, Enterprise Nation has grown into a community of over 75,000 homegrown businesses that find help and support on its website, in its books and at live events. In 2011, the company gave away over £10,000 in funding to UK start-ups, and has recently launched a premium membership scheme, which helps its members promote their businesses and take them to the next level.

Emma is also a co-founder of StartUp Britain, a national campaign to encourage more people to start a business.

Emma was awarded an MBE for services to enterprise in July 2012.

# FOREWORD BY JULIA GOODWIN

HOW DO YOU turn a passion into a business? At *House Beautiful* we hear all the time from talented and creative readers who have an eye for style and design and, having decorated and furnished their own homes, would love to take that talent further afield than their own front door.

If that sounds familiar, then this book is for you. We've combined forces with author Emma Jones to bring you an inspired yet down-to-earth guide to help you achieve your dream. Inside we feature 12 case studies of individuals who have successfully turned a hobby or interest into a business that they love. Now their own bosses, within these pages they share the stories of their journeys, from low-key beginnings to booming and all-absorbing business success stories.

And you can do it too! As well as reading these inspirational success stories, take advantage of author Emma Jones's impressive expertise, as she takes you step-by-step through the practical and legal aspects of setting up on your own, as well as offering insider tips and advice along the way. Armed with all this knowledge, you'll have the tools you need to follow in the footsteps of someone like Jenny McCabe, who set up her handprinted and handmade textiles business Coo & Co, or Sonia Mundey who had a lucky break that kickstarted her interior design business Yellow Book Interiors.

What's interesting is how many of the entrepreneurs featured made use of social media – Blogspot, Facebook, Twitter and Pinterest – to spread the word about their enterprise – and how Etsy and Folksy helped some to make their first sales. And the good news about this method of communication, of course, is that it is free, saving you valuable financial resources that you can divert into other areas of the business.

There's never been a better time to set up on your own – and you can begin in a small way, using your evenings and weekends to develop your skill or product and test the market.

Every month in *House Beautiful* we feature stories of readers who have done just that.

So whether you style, sew, knit, paint or collect unusual pieces, use this guide to help you take the next step – and you may also see the story of your passion for interiors featured in the pages of *House Beautiful*!

*Julia Goodwin*
*Editor,* House Beautiful *Magazine*

# Free eBook edition for all readers

As a buyer of the printed book of *A House Beautiful Home Business*, you can download the full eBook free of charge. Simply point your smartphone or tablet camera at this QR code or go to: **ebooks.harriman-house.com/housebeautiful**

# INTRODUCTION BY EMMA JONES

If you've picked up this book, you'll be thinking about turning a hobby or passion into a business and becoming your own boss. And there's never been a better time to do so!

You can start a business by doing what I call 'working 5 to 9' which is keeping hold of the day job and building the company at nights and weekends. It's a sensible way to start as you keep the security of a salary whilst building confidence and cash flow in the business. Start-up costs are at an all-time low as you can borrow and barter the basic essentials required to get going, and embrace free and low-cost technology tools, such as social media, to grow.

This explains why record numbers of people are moving from employment to self-employment, with a record 484,000 new companies formed in the UK in 2012. They are relishing the freedom and flexibility that comes with being your own boss, as well as the thrill of securing new customers, taking the business global, and creating new products and services.

If this is the kind of working life you're after, simply follow the steps offered in this book and be inspired by the stories of those who have gone before you. In doing so, you will have made a start on your own entrepreneurial journey; I can guarantee it will be one filled with discovery and constant adventure!

*Emma Jones*
emma@enterprisenation.com | @emmaljones

Emma Jones is founder of small business support company Enterprise Nation **www.enterprisenation.com** and a co-founder of StartUp Britain **www.startupbritain.org**.

Enterprise Nation provides daily content, books, eBooks, kits and funding to help anyone start and grow a small business.

# WHO IS THIS BOOK FOR?

THIS BOOK IS for anyone who has a passion, skill or hobby for interiors, furnishings or craft, and an interest in turning this into a business. You may be creating personalised cushions for friends and family and dreaming of doing this full time. You may have a way with putting a room together that could be turned into a successful business. Maybe you paint or draw and wonder if those who offer praise would be prepared to pay for your creations, or whether your flair for home accessories could lead to a financial return.

Whatever your talent, it's likely you can turn this into a business with customers paying for the quality products or services you offer. In this book, you will discover how to:

- make sales beyond friends and family

- promote your brand and become well-known

- register the company and manage the finances

- embrace technology to save time and money

- convey a professional image, online and off

- create a support network and work with partners.

Above all, this book shows you how to make money from doing what you love!

The book is divided into clear chapters with stories throughout of people who have successfully started and grown their own business. They all offer their top tips for success.

With clear steps, useful links and expert advice throughout, consider this book your trusty guide as you go about turning your talent into a business!

# CONTRIBUTORS

With thanks to the following people who have contributed their expertise or story to this book:

## CASE STUDIES

Jenny McCabe – Coo & Co. • Kate Jones & Stephen Gillies – Gillies Jones Glass • Katey Korzenietz – Home Restyler • Sonia Mundey – Yellow Book Interiors • Michelle Grey – Luxury Interiors | Kool Kids Rooms • Rachael Taylor • Lou Gardner – The Vintage Twist Company • Caroline Taylor – Patchwork Harmony | *91 Magazine* • Cheryl Courtney – The Sewing Room • James and Sally Tickner – Liberty Rose Interiors • Billy Lloyd – Billy Lloyd Ceramics • Emily Readett-Bayley – Emily Readett-Bayley Ltd. | POSH Graffiti® | POSH Salvage™ • Kate Schuricht – Kate Schuricht Ceramics

## EXPERTS

Emily Coltman, FreeAgent • Joanne Dewberry, Charlie Moo's • Louise Findlay-Wilson, PRPro • Cally Robson, She's Ingenious • Mark Shaw, Twitter expert • Greg Simpson, Press For Attention • Jackie Wade, Winning Sales • Laura Rigney, Pitcher House • Mark and Philomena, Business Photography • Niamh Guckian, Totally Wired

## HOUSE BEAUTIFUL CONTRIBUTORS

Julia Goodwin • Julia Evans • Zoe Jobson

We would also like to say a special thanks to Caroline Taylor of Patchwork Harmony for her invaluable help and assistance in putting this book together.

# Chapter One
## MAKING THE MOVE FROM HOBBY TO
# BUSINESS

# COMING UP WITH AN IDEA

WHEN STARTING A new business, the first step is to come up with an idea. What will the business do? What skills of yours will it use? What talents will give it an advantage over others?

Whether you're struggling to define your idea, or are overwhelmed by too many, often the most important thing to bear in mind is that a *niche* business can be the best kind of business.

What I mean by this is: come up with a product or service that meets the needs of a very well-defined audience. For example, Liberty Rose Interiors and The Vintage Twist Company.

There are two key benefits to having a niche business:

1. You keep marketing costs low, as your audience is very specific; you know where to find them and you have researched and understand the kind of marketing messages to which they will respond.

2. Customer loyalty remains high, as you become the expert in your field or the only provider of certain products to your market.

Think about how you can fashion your talent into an idea that has a clear purpose for a clearly defined audience.

Base your business on what you enjoy making but with an eye on what people will buy.

## Researching the market

Research your potential customers, the competition and a price point by visiting competitors' sites, online trade sites and forums, reading reports, and seeking intelligence from experts. Use survey tools such as SurveyMonkey (**www.surveymonkey.com**) and Wufoo (**www.wufoo.com**), and pose questions on Twitter, Facebook and LinkedIn.

Look for information that will answer the following questions:

- What is the number of potential customers you can serve, and how do these customers like to be served?

- What are their characteristics, spending patterns and who are their key influencers?

- Who is currently serving your market?

- Where are your potential customers going for their goods and services?

- What do they like about what they're getting and, more importantly, what do they dislike (as this opens up opportunities for you to improve on the status quo)?

In view of the above, is there a business here? Is there room in the market for your product or service and is the demand there?

If so, you then need to start thinking about what price you can charge.

*"Make sure you understand the market you want to enter, research your competitors – why are they or aren't they doing well?"*

– Katey Korzenietz, Home Restyler

*"Do your research at the start. Immerse yourself in the industry, find out what it is people want and consider if what you have to offer really fits in with the market."*

– Caroline Taylor, Patchwork Harmony

Price yourself at a rate that's competitive with other providers in the market, that takes into account the amount of time, personal service and added value you offer, and that will turn a profit at the end of the day!

## SURVEY TOOLS

- SurveyMonkey | **www.surveymonkey.com**

- Wufoo | **www.wufoo.com**

Carry out research face-to-face by displaying goods at fairs and markets and complete the market research template below to be sure there's a sufficient market of people to buy your products at a price that will turn a profit.

# Market research template

**How big is the market?**

*What is the number of potential customers I can serve and how do these customers like to be served?*

..................................................................................................................
..................................................................................................................
..................................................................................................................

*What are their characteristics, spending patterns and who are their key influences?*

..................................................................................................................
..................................................................................................................
..................................................................................................................

**Who is currently serving my market?**

*Where are my potential customers going for their goods and services?*

..................................................................................................................
..................................................................................................................
..................................................................................................................

*What do they like about what they're getting, and, more importantly, what do they dislike?*

..................................................................................................................
..................................................................................................................
..................................................................................................................

**What price can I charge for my product/service?**

*What's competitive and takes into account the amount of time, personal service and added value that I offer?*

...........................................................................................................

...........................................................................................................

...........................................................................................................

# Friends and family focus group

When moving from hobby to business, friends and family represent a key focus group and will often be your most ardent supporters. Talk through your ideas and ask for feedback on the product/service itself and your qualities in being able to deliver. Joanne Dewberry rightly says that you should test products on strangers too, but conversations with friends and family will help you prepare an initial SWOT analysis for the business.

# SWOT Analysis

With your idea and research in hand, prepare a SWOT analysis. This stands for: Strengths, Weaknesses, Opportunities, Threats.

## STRENGTHS

**What are my strengths?**

What can I do better than anyone else?

What resources do I have?

What's my unique selling point?

## OPPORTUNITIES

**What opportunities do I see?**

Does my idea tap into any trends?

Are there any emerging technologies that could help my idea?

Has there been anything in the news related to my idea?

## WEAKNESSES

**What are my weaknesses?**

What should I avoid?

Where do I lack skills?

What might hinder my success?

## THREATS

**What threats would I face?**

Who's my competition?

Does changing technology affect my idea?

TIP { **What am I worth?**

How much do you think customers or clients would pay for your product or service? To begin with, take a look at how similar offerings are priced and talk to your potential customers about how much they'd be willing to pay. Then talk to potential suppliers to check you can source materials and deliver at a price that covers your costs and still leaves a margin for that all-important profit.

Since starting a business from home will save you lots of money, you can pass some of these savings onto your customers, which could give you an edge over other businesses. However, make sure you don't undercharge for the expertise, talent and knowledge you offer, as this is all part of the product people are buying.

Also consider charging less for work that will reflect well on your business and boost your reputation, perhaps in the media or with a credible customer.

*James and Sally Tickner carried out market research when they wanted to take their business to the next level . . .*

# BEAUTIFUL BUSINESS: LIBERTY ROSE INTERIORS

**Name:** James and Sally Tickner, Liberty Rose Interiors Limited

**Business:** Furnishings and upholstery

**Website:** www.libertyroseinteriors.co.uk

**Social media:** www.libertyroseinteriors.blogspot.co.uk, www.pinterest.com/LibertyRoseUK, www.facebook.com/LibertyRoseInteriorsLimited, @libertyrose

Liberty Rose Interiors Limited was established in spring 2012 by husband-and-wife team James and Sally Tickner. James began life in the upholstery industry over 20 years ago and has been passionately revitalising furniture by hand ever since. He has also worked in the leather-trimming business to transform the interiors of many luxury yachts, helicopters and classic cars. Sally has been in the book-publishing business for most of her career and is a self-confessed spendaholic!

> "We bought an old house and tried new influences and styles – Jim created some chairs for our lounge which were the envy of our friends so we decided to design and create our own pieces to suit a contemporary home and we looked for a way to sell them."

Like many new businesses they initially struggled to think of a suitable name for themselves but after much discussion they decided to use their daughter's name, Liberty Rose.

> "When she entered our lives the one name we agreed upon (and there were many!) was Liberty Rose and the meaning of it seems to fit with the aim and scope of our business – *Liberty* means the power of choosing, thinking and acting for oneself, and a bed of *roses* is a situation of comfort or ease. In our minds, Liberty Rose is about taking something precious such as a much-loved antique chair and revitalising it – boldly choosing something exquisite which will provide comfort (and hopefully fun, passion and warmth) for years to follow."

Liberty Rose sold their first piece to a friend! "We were having dinner at their place and they mentioned that their sofa was in need of a complete makeover. The next day they asked us to submit a quote, which we did. This then prompted us to map out a business plan and to start to think about how to generate new opportunities."

Like many new businesses, when James and Sally initially decided to go for it, they had big dreams combined with little time and money. As a result, they created a basic marketing plan for the initial phase and worked with a friend to design an effective website to showcase their collection.

"In particular, we highlighted some 'before and after' pictures of a sofa transformation to demonstrate the traditional methods we use. Our original website was simple and has been easy to maintain, so we update that regularly and also use social media sites such as Facebook, Twitter and Pinterest to inform people of our latest news."

However, they soon realised that they needed to offer potential customers a way to see for themselves how their portfolio was different from the normal foam-filled chairs and sofas found on the high street. They considered a number of ways to do this.

"We looked for a showroom in a prime location where we could feature our range of products and promote our upholstery service. After some market research we found The Packhouse, a destination lifestyle centre located in a 400-year old Grade II listed former hop kiln, on the outskirts of Farnham, Surrey. We rent a showroom and benefit from their sales and marketing abilities, which enables us to create fresh pieces for our collection, expand our supply chain and develop additional channels to market, with an emphasis on social media."

In order to grow the business, James and Sally started to think more commercially about their products and services and also researched what their competitors were doing.

"We allocated time to visit leading high atreet stores and registered for trade fairs and assessed how to position ourselves as being better than the mass market items."

As part of that, they considered their ethos and values and decided to focus on how to reflect that in their communication with customers.

"We decided to only use the very best high-quality fabrics, to raise awareness of the traditional and ethical upholstery methods we adopt (such as our use of horsehair) and we pride ourselves on delivering a friendly and professional service."

Within a few months they also started to look for adjacent business opportunities to grow their business and reflect their values. They sourced a range of homeware items that complemented their collection, including silver lanterns, bespoke tables, hand-sewn floor cushions, vintage vases and pictures, and negotiated the costs to fit with their low start-up budget.

> "We were also keen to build a strong brand for ourselves so we worked with a designer to create some logos and developed ways to package our smaller items. For our first Christmas we worked with a supplier to create a range of clean wax (no lead) candles and diffusers which used high quality fragrance oil that was pure and undiluted. We also commissioned our own packaging to reflect the Liberty Rose Interiors logo and style and were delighted with the results."

At this stage in their business, Sally and James are keen to increase sales in their local market before taking their business global. However, they have started to look into the options and intend to assess the opportunities at a later date. 2013 will also see them develop new and innovative products, as well as testing new products in the form of high quality wallpapers, rugs and paints.

# Top tips!

1. "Look to your passion for inspiration. We are passionate about our products and services and we share that with our customers."

2. "Consider your values and vision and look for ways to communicate that. Our ethos is simple. It's about celebrating individual vision. We provide our friends and customers (same thing!) with furniture that they won't find in anyone else's home because it is totally unique to them."

3. "Engage with your customers and allow them to influence your decisions. We use social networking channels to talk directly to our customers; we ask questions about where they shop and we are eager to understand their likes and dislikes regarding colours, fabrics and textures. We treat our customers as individuals. We genuinely want to create statement pieces that will add *va va voom* to their homes."

4. "Prioritise what will make you money. In the early days it's easy to get distracted from your core business. We attempt to limit the time we spend on emails, we avoid long visits from sales reps, we design and create our own products whenever we can and we actively look for reciprocal marketing opportunities and free publicity."

5. "Evaluate your business on a regular basis, be flexible about what isn't working and be prepared to change We understand what is selling and we are honest about anything that isn't. We only buy things that we are passionate about, we test the market and we avoid overstocking. For anyone considering starting up a soft furnishing and upholstery business it's important to understand interior design trends, to be an ambassador for your own products and services and above all, to be energetic and open to new ideas, even the crazy ones!"

# The name game

Coming up with an idea and carrying out research will get you thinking about what to name your new baby (by which I mean your business!). If you are selling your services or your knowledge the company may be named after you, for example, 'Emma Jones Interior Design', in which case, job done. But if that's not appropriate, think of a name that:

* is easy to spell

* is not already registered with Companies House (you can use a free web-check service to access existing company names at **www.companieshouse.gov.uk**) or trademarked

* people will remember

* has an available domain name.

You might want to protect the name with a trademark to make sure that no one else can take it in the future.

If you get stuck, visit Enterprise Nation (**www.enterprisenation.com**) where you will find people who can help you win the name game, as the site is buzzing with talented copywriters and wordsmiths.

*Sonia Mundey named her company Yellow Book Interiors after taking inspiration from a 19th century quarterly . . .*

# BEAUTIFUL BUSINESS: YELLOW BOOK INTERIORS

**Name:** Sonia Mundey

**Business:** Yellow Book Interiors Ltd

**Website:** www.yellowbookinteriors.co.uk

**Social media:** www.facebook.com/pages/Yellow-Book-Interiors-Ltd/111090695681888

Sonia Mundey's business journey began in 2011, shortly after her son's first birthday.

> "I had worked in the interior design business for five years, working with private clients, as well as show home and hotel refurbishment projects, but had wanted to work for myself for some time."

After completing a degree in History of Art at Birkbeck, University of London, Sonia began to seriously consider working for herself. She loved the idea of combining her love of interior design with her knowledge of art history and creating something amazing. Shortly after, interior design business Yellow Book Interiors was born. She hasn't looked back since!

When looking for her business name, Sonia was inspired by *The Yellow Book*, a cultural quarterly published in the 1890s that was renowned for highlighting beautiful art and the creative energy of the age.

> "Our outlook is firmly 21st century, but just like the original *Yellow Book* we're always looking for beautiful ways to brighten everyday life."

Yellow Book Interiors' first customer came through word of mouth.

> "A family friend who is a builder and developer got in touch and asked me to refurbish his Grade II listed cottage near Blandford, Dorset, which was a great start to the business."

Since then, Sonia has promoted the business through her website, as well using social media and local advertising.

"We are a part of Home Welcome packs which are given to people who have just moved house in the Bournemouth/Poole/New Forest area."

Promotional postcards and word of mouth also help Sonia to get the word out about her business.

Yellow Book Interiors is run solely by Sonia but she has started to develop a strong network of reliable trades and suppliers.

"Working with local trades and suppliers has proved to be a very worthwhile experience. As well as helping to support local businesses it has also meant that I can negotiate better terms and discounts with them. By meeting with people face-to-face you can foster a much better relationship and have far better bargaining power with them. You can also share your knowledge and expertise much more personally than just dealing with companies over the phone. Modern technology is wonderful but there is no substitute for human contact!"

Following a very successful first year in business, Sonia has big plans for the next 12 months.

"I'd like to develop relationships with local estate agents, and I hope to offer a home-styling service for people who are looking to sell their homes at the best possible price."

## Top tip!

"Just go for it! Have confidence in your own ability, be conscientious and pro-active and it will happen!"

# 6 tips for launching a homemade craft business

*Joanne Dewberry, founder of Charlie Moo's (***www.charliemoos.co.uk***) and author of* Crafting a Successful Small Business *(***www.enterprisenation.com/shop/craftingasuccessfulsmallbusiness***) provides her top tips for launching a homemade craft business . . .*

1. "Start with something you know (you can develop other skills behind the scenes). This way you can be confident and know the products are of a suitable quality."

2. "Decide where you will sell, whether that's on or offline, craft fairs and/or websites."

3. "Research what others are making, where they sell, the prices they sell at and how they are branded and marketed. Find out if you need any information on your products' packaging. Do they need testing? Do you need any certification? Food or natural products will need ingredients listing, kitchens will need to be inspected by environmental health, toys will need CE testing for health and safety. Make sure you know all of this."

4. "Pricing is vital. You have to take everything into consideration; factor in waste, shipping, equipment, advertising, utilities such as the internet, electricity, telephones, time and your hourly wage."

5. "Test the market. Get your products in front of others. Find out what they like, don't like etc. Talk to family members, bearing in mind they are normally well meaning and may not provide the helpful criticism you need so test on strangers too – a market is a good starting place."

6. "Have fun – that's why you started in the first place!"

# The franchise option

Consider buying into a franchise or direct-selling opportunity that enables you to develop your skills whilst being self-employed and benefiting from being part of an entrepreneurial team that provides you with templates, branding, training and help with finances.

Whether your passion is beautiful homewares or you have a passion for all things gardening, there's a franchise opportunity out there for you. A couple are listed here; you can find more in *50 Fantastic Franchises* (**www.enterprisenation.com/shop/50fantasticfranchises**).

- Jamie at Home (**www.jamieathome.com**) – perfect for anyone with an interest in kitchen and dining accessories. Sales events are held in the homes of friends and their network.

- Girlie Gardening (**www.girliegardening.com**) – green fingers, step forward! Become a Girlie Gardening franchise and you'll be selling Welly Warmers and gardening gloves to those who spend ample time in the herbaceous borders!

- Neal's Yard Remedies (**www.nyrorganic.com**) – if selling organic natural health and beauty products is your idea of heaven, this is the opportunity you've been waiting for.

# Chapter Two
## PLANNING YOUR
# BUSINESS

# BUSINESS PLAN

AFTER COMING UP with an idea and doing your research, writing a brief business plan is your first practical step to starting your business. A business plan will act as your map; it will guide the business from start to growth, with reference to milestones along the way. For example, you might want to open a shop, launch a website or reach a number of customers within a certain time frame. And, of course, you'll need to refer to resources: what you have already, what you'll need and how you'll pay for it.

You will need a plan if you're looking to raise money, from friends or family or from the bank. But it's a very important document even if you aren't looking for external funds just yet.

With it in hand, you'll be off on your business journey. "I'm off!" you might say.

Or IMOFF.

It's an easy way to remember the headings to include in your business plan: Idea, Market, Operations, Financials and Friends.

- **Idea:** What's your idea?
- **Market:** Who will be your customers or clients? And who is your competition?
- **Operations:** How will you develop the idea, promote it, and provide good customer service?
- **Financials:** Can you earn more than you spend, so that the business makes a profit? Do you need any funds to get started?
- **Friends:** Do you have a support network on hand for when you need business advice? Are there complementary businesses you've identified with whom partnerships are a possibility?

Have these as headings in your plan and you've taken a big step closer to becoming your own boss.

TIP { **Revisit regularly**

Review your plan regularly to check progress against targets or to make changes as you respond to new opportunities. I revisit the Enterprise Nation plan for a 'gentle' recap every six months and then at the start of each year head off for a couple of days to re-read the plan, rethink the business, and rewrite if required.

Here are the headings of a detailed business plan template you can complete and call your own . . .

EXECUTIVE SUMMARY

THE IDEA

THE MARKET

Customers

COMPETITION

Operations

The CEO

Sourcing

SALES & MARKETING

Press

Online

Partners

Systems

FRIENDS & FAMILY

FINANCIALS

# Chapter Three
## THE MUST-DO'S

# REGISTERING THE COMPANY

A S THE BUSINESS comes into being, so does a duty to register the company as a trading entity. There's also the company assets to consider (brand/name/idea) and how to protect them.

## Register the company

When you set up in business there is one key organisation to contact and inform: HM Revenue & Customs (HMRC). You may also need to register with Companies House. You can get help to do this from Companies Made Simple (**www.companiesmadesimple.com**), an award-winning company formation agent.

However, before contacting either HMRC or Companies House, have a think about the company status that suits you best. There are a number of options:

### SELF-EMPLOYED

As it sounds, self-employed means working for yourself; you keep records and accounts of your own activity, and, in acting alone, get to keep all the profits – but are also solely liable for any debts.

If you set up as a self-employed sole trader you don't need to register with Companies House or take on any of the accounting duties that come with being a limited company (outlined below).

### PARTNERSHIP

If you'd like to be self-employed but want to work with a friend or colleague, consider a partnership. It means that two or more people share the risks, costs, profits and workload.

Partnerships do not have to file accounts at Companies House but there are filing requirements with HMRC. A limited liability partnership or LLP is structured in the same way as a normal partnership but, as it sounds, limits the liability of each partner. An LLP has the same filing requirements at Companies House as a limited company.

## LIMITED COMPANY

Limited companies exist in their own right, with the company's finances kept separate from the personal finances of its owner(s).

Limited companies have filing responsibilities with both Companies House and HMRC as noted below but it's now much easier to launch a limited company as there is no longer a need to appoint a company secretary, so you can be a limited company with a headcount of one, which many small businesses are!

### TIP { Take advice

The status of your company will affect how much admin you have to do and the kind of financial records you must keep and file. Take advice from your accountant or local tax office on which one to choose as much depends on the type of business you will be running.

# Being social

Should you decide to start a social enterprise – a business trading for social and environmental purposes – there are additional legal structures to consider, including:

- community interest company (CIC)

- industrial and provident society

- charitable status.

To find out more about launching a social enterprise or creating a community interest company (CIC) visit:

- Social Enterprise | **www.socialenterprise.org.uk**
- CIC Regulator | **www.cicregulator.gov.uk**

TIP { A friendly guide to legal structure

Check out GOV.UK's friendly guide to the best legal structure for your business at: **www.gov.uk/business-legal-structures**

# Companies House

When registering with Companies House there are two options from which to choose. You can buy a 'ready-made' company from a company formation agent, such as Companies Made Simple, who form a company on your behalf for a fee of £16.99 and in three hours, or 'incorporate' a company yourself by sending documents and a registration fee to Companies House. If you decide to complete registration yourself, download the form from **bit.ly/ezw1S**.

# HM Revenue & Customs

The rules on registering a new business with HM Revenue & Customs are pretty clear-cut. You are required to register as soon as you start earning from any business activity. As above, you can choose to register as self-employed, as a partnership, or as a limited company. Each category has its own filing requirements, as outlined below.

## SOLE TRADER/SELF-EMPLOYED

The calculation of tax due and National Insurance owing is done through self-assessment.

You either need to complete form CWF1 or call the newly self-employed business helpline. This should be done within three months of undertaking your first piece of self-employed work in order to avoid a fine.

- Form CWF₁ | **www.hmrc.gov.uk/forms/cwf1.pdf**
- Helpline for the newly self-employed | 0845 915 4515

It's not onerous to complete the form and, once registered, you'll be classified as self-employed and sent a self-assessment tax return each year, which you complete, showing your income and expenses from self-employment as well as details of your employment elsewhere (if applicable).

You will be subject to tax and National Insurance on any profits you make, but the good news is that any losses incurred can be offset against your employed income (if you have any), which could even result in a tax rebate.

Depending on your turnover and how straightforward your tax affairs are, you may be able to complete the Short Tax Return (SA200). However, this cannot be self-selected, nor is it on the HMRC website; HMRC will send it to you automatically if they think you qualify, based on information given in the previous year's return. If you have turnover below £68,000, it's likely that you will qualify. As ever, though, it will depend on individual circumstances, and the law (and various criteria it uses) may change!

Self-assessment tax return deadlines are as follows:

- paper tax returns should be received by HMRC by 31 October of tax year ending 5 April.
- online tax returns should be completed by 31 January (giving you an extra three months).

## USEFUL LINKS

- 'Thinking of working for yourself?' | **www.hmrc.gov.uk/leaflets/se1.pdf**
- Helping you understand self-assessment and your tax return | **www.hmrc.gov.uk/sa**

## PARTNERSHIP

According to HMRC, a partnership is where:

> "Two or more people set up a business. Each partner is personally responsible for all the business debts, even if the debt was caused by another partner. As partners, each pays income

tax on their share of the business profits through self-assessment, as well as National Insurance."

In terms of filing requirements, each partner should complete a partnership supplementary page as part of their individual self-assessment tax return. This is in addition to a partnership return, which has to be submitted by one nominated partner and show each partner's share of profits/losses.

The deadlines for partnership tax returns are as follows:

- paper tax returns should be received by HMRC by 31 October of tax year ending 5 April

- online tax returns should be completed by 31 January (giving you an extra three months).

## LIMITED COMPANY

As mentioned, a limited company's finances are distinct from the finances of their owner(s). What this means is that the company is liable for its own debts, not the individual owners, as is the case if you are self-employed or in a partnership. As mentioned earlier, you can form a new limited company by registering with Companies House (**www.companieshouse.gov.uk**) or by using a company creation agent.

As well as registering with Companies House, you also need to let HMRC know you are operating as a limited company. You can do this by completing form CT41G.

You will also need to set up and register a PAYE scheme as you are an employee of the company.

- Register PAYE scheme | **www.hmrc.gov.uk/newemployers**

- New employer's helpline | 0845 60 70 143

In terms of filing requirements, you must complete a self-assessment company tax return at the end of the accounting period. The return will show the company's taxable profits and whether any corporation tax is owed, and can be filed online at **www.hmrc.gov.uk/ct**. The return should also be filed with Companies House to comply with the Companies Act 2006. This can be done free of charge, using their online WebFiling: **ewf.companieshouse.gov.uk**

On your returns, you can claim wear-and-tear allowances (capital allowances) on any work-related equipment you buy, and also an element of your expenses for working from home. You can also claim travelling expenses, subsistence and a proportion of your phone calls.

Visit the 'Claim Income Tax reliefs' section on the GOV.UK website to view the tax allowances, deductions and reliefs you can claim: **www.gov.uk/income-tax-reliefs**

Company tax returns must be filed within 12 months of the end of your company's corporation tax accounting period. More details on these deadlines can be found at: **www.hmrc.gov.uk/ ct/getting-started/deadlines.htm**

# In good order

Keep records of your business dealings – this will make it much easier to complete tax returns when the time comes. Keep hold of:

- receipts of business-related purchases
- copies of invoices to customers
- bank statements (especially if you don't have a separate account for the business)
- utility bills (if you are starting the business from home and using part of the house for business); they can be claimed as a business expense and so reduce your tax bill.

For advice from HMRC on good record keeping, visit: **www.hmrc.gov.uk/startingup/ keeprecs.htm**

If you plan to do your tax returns yourself rather than using an accountant, consider taking a workshop which will help with your understanding of the process: **www.hmrc.gov.uk/bst/advice-team-events/work1.htm**

# VAT

Whichever tax status you choose, if your business turns over more than a certain amount (always check the latest level), or you think your turnover will soon exceed this amount, you must also register for value added tax (VAT).

You can voluntarily register at any time. Being VAT-registered can bring credibility with certain customers, but adding VAT to your invoices may make you more expensive than competitors and you will have to file a VAT return four times a year.

- How and when to register for VAT | **www.hmrc.gov.uk/vat/start/register**

# Accountant accompaniment

Talk to a qualified accountant about the structure that is best for your business. And consider employing their services to complete your tax returns. Even if your accounts are very simple, it is well worth seeking professional advice, particularly as the rules and regulations can change frequently and without warning.

Find an accountant by visiting:

- ICAEW (Institute of Chartered Accountants in England and Wales) | **www.icaew.com**

- List of Sage-accredited professionals | **www.sage.co.uk/partner**

- Accountant partners of online software tool FreeAgent | **www.freeagentcentral.com/partners**

Enterprise Nation has an online marketplace of business service providers: **www.enterprisenation.com/directory**

## USEFUL LINKS

- Starting a Business | **www.hmrc.gov.uk/startingup**

- GOV.UK on business tax | **www.gov.uk/browse/business/business-tax**

# Business rates

The final form of tax to bear in mind is business rates. If you have applied for planning permission or your local authority is aware you are running a business from home, they may try to charge you business rates as opposed to council tax on the part of the house being used for business purposes. Business rates are different in each area and something that should be discussed with your local authority.

• GOV.UK on business rates | **www.gov.uk/introduction-to-business-rates**

# HOUSEHOLD ADMIN

With a business plan prepared and the regulatory bodies informed, it's time to take care of the household admin and make friends with the neighbours!

Over 60% of businesses are started from home on account of the low costs and lack of commute. When you start and grow your business from home, you may have a few questions about who you need to inform. Here are the answers.

### Q: DO I NEED PLANNING PERMISSION?

**A:** You'll need planning permission to base the business at home if you answer 'yes' to any of these questions:

• will your home no longer be used mainly as a private residence?

• will your business result in a marked rise in traffic or people calling?

• will your business involve any activities that are unusual in a residential area?

• will your business disturb the neighbours at unreasonable hours or create other forms of nuisance such as noise or smells?

If your house is pretty much going to remain a house, with your business quietly accommodated within it, then permission shouldn't be required. If you're unsure, contact your local council (**www.planningportal.gov.uk**) to seek their views.

## Q: DO I NEED TO TELL THE LOCAL AUTHORITY I'M WORKING FROM HOME?

**A:** This depends on whether you pass the planning test. If you need planning permission, you'll have to inform your local authority. If you don't, then the only benefit of telling them is that they'll charge you business rates (rather than council tax) on the part of the house being used for business purposes. Business rates are different in each area and something that should be discussed with your local authority.

## Q: DO I NEED TO TELL THE LANDLORD?

**A:** Yes, it's best to let them know that you will be working from home. The good news is that the coalition government announced on 1 November 2010 that social landlords should review any contracts prohibiting people from running a business from home.

## Q: DO I NEED TO INFORM MY MORTGAGE PROVIDER?

**A:** Yes, it's best to let them know – even though it shouldn't mean any change in the mortgage repayment.

## Q: WHAT ABOUT MY INSURANCE PROVIDER? DO THEY NEED TO KNOW?

**A:** Yes, do inform your insurance company. Tell them about the equipment and stock you have at home. An upgrade from domestic to a business policy is not usually expensive so don't be put off in making this call. Your insurance provider is likely to recommend that you also take out public liability insurance in case anyone who comes to visit suffers an injury in or around your home office. See the next section for details of the type of insurance you may need.

## Q: DO I NEED PROTECTION FOR WHEN CUSTOMERS AND CONTACTS COME TO VISIT?

**A:** Yes, carry out a health and safety check, which is easy to do by following the steps set out by the Health and Safety Executive in their homeworking guide (PDF available at **www.hse.gov.uk/pubns/indg226.pdf**).

## Q: SHOULD I TELL THE NEIGHBOURS?

**A:** Yes. When working from home it's worth keeping your neighbours sweet and firmly on side. You don't want them getting annoyed by any deliveries or unusual distractions. If that's a risk, tell them about your business, always give advance warnings, and don't be slow to ask them to business parties and events to thank them for their patience.

# Get insured

There are different categories of insurance which you need to know about to secure the policy that's right for you. The main ones are:

- **Professional indemnity** – relevant to businesses offering services and knowledge and provides protection if you receive a claim alleging a negligent act, error or omission committed by you in the course of the conduct of your professional business.

- **Public liability** – advisable to have if clients are visiting your home office and/or you are supplying goods to consumers. This will protect you in the event of potential injury to business visitors and/or damages arising from the supply or sale of goods which have caused injury to a third party or their property. Public liability insurance is also needed if you plan to sell your wares at markets or events. Many organisers will ask to see this before granting you a stall.

- **Business interruption** – covers your potential loss of revenue following a material damage loss.

- **Employer's liability** – only applies when you have employees and offers protection in the event of death or injury to them sustained in the course of their employment.

- **Motor insurance** – This is different to standard car insurance, which does not include business use. If you have a vehicle dedicated for business use to carry stock and/or products, you should buy motor insurance or get a business extension on your car insurance policy when using your existing car for business travel.

- **Home insurance** – You are likely to already have a home insurance policy but this will generally not cover business activities carried out at home or business equipment within the home. Speak to your insurance provider and upgrade to a business policy. This is not usually costly but it will ensure you're protected.

# Chapter Four

## BUILDING AND PROTECTING YOUR BRAND

# YOUR BUSINESS'S FIRST IMPRESSION

A S SOON AS you begin to think about products, you need to start thinking about your brand. Your brand will tie everything you do together: from what you sell to how you sell it. It will determine product ranges, packaging, your online presence – just about everything.

It leaves your business's first impression on every customer, supplier and partner. Here's some advice on how to make sure that impression is a good one.

## Look at my logo!

Customers will get an immediate sense of your style from your logo and related branding. Impress with a nice-looking company design that's repeated across promotional materials, from business cards to brochures.

Think about what you'd like as your company font, colours and layout. Have a go at designing this yourself or hire the services of a designer/neighbour/friend. Good presentation can make a world of difference. And it may just be the difference you need to clinch a client.

Check out free and funky fonts at **www.fontsquirrel.com**, and logo blogs like **www.underconsideration.com/brandnew**, for inspiration.

Find a professional to design your logo via these sites:

- CrowdSPRING | **www.crowdspring.com**
- 99 designs | **www.99designs.com**
- Enterprise Nation | **www.enterprisenation.com/directory**
- Concept Cupboard | **www.conceptcupboard.com**
- BuildaBrand | **www.buildabrand.com**

# Business cards

It used to be a bit of a palaver to get business cards printed, as well as expensive. First there was a designer to brief, then you had to order a thousand at a time and they often took weeks to arrive. These days you can pop into most stationers, tell them what you want and they can print a set in minutes, while you wait – or you can come back later to collect. Or order online via the links below. Use this opportunity to show off your flair . . .

- MOO | **www.moo.com**
- Printing.com | **www.printing.com**
- Vistaprint | **www.vistaprint.co.uk**
- Staples copy and print centres | **www.staples.co.uk/copy-print**

Richard Moross, founder of MOO.com, says:

> "The point of having a business card is to make a connection, create a relationship and leave something with the recipient that reminds them of you. Have cards that tell a story. Use that card as a sales tool, for sure, but also show appreciation by having cards relating to your customer."

Richard Moross achieves this by having images on his cards showing places he's visited and meals he's eaten. With 70% of MOO's business being outside the UK, Richard travels a lot and the cards act as an ice-breaker in meetings as he tells the story behind the pictures.

TIP { Get pinned to a fridge

Always include a business card or flyer with your online or in person sales. The customer may stick it to their fridge, for example, and your brand will forever be in their vision and remind them to come back to you!

# Promotional flyers

Getting your message to as many people as possible is key. Flyers are a cheap and quick way to do this. Stationery stores can normally print about 1,000 A5 flyers in half an hour while you wait – a cost-effective way to get your brand in front of people.

Increase your chances of turning flyers into firm sales by:

• having a design that is memorable, possibly quirky and, ideally, that your potential customers will want to keep on their desktop/in their purse/atop the kitchen shelf

• making the offer clear and confirming the benefits of buying

• including a call to action, i.e. a way in which the interested customer can contact you.

# BEAUTIFUL BUSINESS: POSH

**Name:** Emily Readett-Bayley

**Business:** Emily Readett-Bayley Ltd. | POSH Graffiti® | POSH Salvage™

**Website:** www.poshgraffiti.com | www.poshsalvage.com

**Social media:** @EmilyReadettB | @POSHGraffiti | www.facebook.com/pages/POSH-Graffiti/40458139472

Emily Readett-Bayley's design business began after a visit to Indonesia in 1989.

"I had studied theatre design at Wimbledon School of Art in London, before visiting Indonesia with a British theatre company who were sourcing and rehearsing in Bali. Commissioning wooden masks and props led me to note the unique skills and beautiful natural materials used and I was encouraged by the people I met."

Emily then decided to explore the opportunity of combining her own design ideas and knowledge of the London Theatre and Arts with the traditional skills she had seen.

"I started with a selection of small woodcarvings, modifications of existing designs I saw whilst working in Bali, most of which drew inspiration from the natural world. I modified the colours, played with scale and selected things which had been beautifully crafted that I thought would sell into quite a sophisticated British market."

She began by exhibiting her products at country fairs and charity fairs which led to her being asked in 1991 to have a stall in a shop in Neal's Yard, Covent Garden.

"My stock sold so well the landlord asked me to join him in a profit share arrangement and run the shop with him. At the same time I also learnt that there were empty shops on the Westminster Estate due to the recession at that time and I opened a pop-up Christmas shop on Newburgh Street, just off Carnaby Street, which I continued every Christmas in various shops until 1996. Many journalists and buyers walked past the shop window and came in to see our products, which meant we began to get press. My first serious trade order was for a range of Christmas decorations for Liberty."

Retailing in central London also meant that Emily could tune into the zeitgeist; she met lots of people and could talk to them about what they were interested in.

"I was first asked if I could produce gilded wooden letters spelling the names of three Vietnamese Rivers by architects working on a restaurant in Fulham and it was another letter commission for a different architect that formed the basis of our Old English POSH Graffiti today."

The sales of the letters were steady throughout the 1990s, but it wasn't until the advent of SMS messaging, Banksy and the internet that sound bites and messaging with text really began to grow.

"By 2003, when we made our company website, other alphabets had appeared at the trade shows and shortly afterwards the name 'posh graffiti' popped into a conversation and we knew that was what we had to call the letters and the decorations that sold with them to distinguish them from factory-made copies."

At this stage, Emily made a clear decision about manufacturing her products and the ethos she wanted to promote.

"I probably could have taken my POSH Graffiti designs to China and may well have made a lot of money quickly, but I knew that in the long term the value of the brand was that our lovely pieces were my original designs hand-carved from a sustainable wood and not manufactured in a huge quantity."

From the beginning, Emily has always taken care to source sustainable materials and for many years has pioneered the concept of stylish design with ethical manufacture, with all of the products made by the same village community in Bali.

Emily has seen the business grow over the last few years thanks to the internet.

"It has slowly enabled us to benefit from the ability to retail online ourselves without the expense or limitations of physical shops. The POSH Graffiti is particularly suited to mail order and there is a global market to be explored. However we still wholesale to other retailers and as I am able to design and manufacture bespoke collections in smallish runs this puts us in a good position to offer them something exclusive. I think it is important to keep the brand out on the shop floor as well as online. Who knows, in the future we may return to retail in central London with our own flagship store!"

Emily has also grown the business with the introduction of complementary items.

"For the practical purposes of shipping containers from Indonesia I have always needed to sell some larger items alongside the POSH Graffiti and my interest in the natural world and eco issues inspired me to make my first bamboo collection which I exhibited alongside the letters and decorations at early trade shows."

As a result, she has built a second brand around these materials, with faux driftwood furniture, salvaged teak tables and bamboo ladders all working alongside the smaller items in the collections. These items now sell under the POSH Salvage brand name, which along with POSH Graffiti sells internationally.

"We retail online of course and sell to the trade via British and international trade shows such as Top Drawer in London and Christmasworld in Frankfurt both of which have a global reach and attract the best buyers in the sector."

Emily now runs the business with her sister, who joined in 1997.

"We have different skills but a similar design ethos and definitely work well as a team."

They are hoping that 2013 will bring growth as they have licensed the POSH Graffiti brand and a new collaboration is allowing Emily to add an exciting new range to POSH Salvage.

"I have been invited to work with an Indonesian/American manufacturing facility to develop a design-led furniture collection for the European market to be sold under the POSH Salvage brand. This utilises waste wood salvaged from landslides and volcanic eruptions in Java and will hopefully lead to an additional partnership in Central Borneo. The Borneo project is part of an important long-term climate change pilot and something in which I'm very interested."

# Office address

If you are running your business from home there are a couple of reasons why you might not want to put the address on your business card: it might sound too domestic for your brand, and you might not want people turning up on your doorstep!

You can solve this with a P.O. Box number, which starts at £185 per year and is easily set up with Royal Mail (**www.royalmail.com/pobox**). Alternatively, you could invest in a virtual office, which gives you a more tailored and personal service than a P.O. Box – plus you get a nice-sounding address and a place to meet clients. Having a virtual office enables you to choose the address that suits you best, have post delivered to that location, and then forwarded on to you. Companies providing this service include:

- Regus | **www.regus.co.uk**
- Mail Boxes Etc. | **www.mbe.co.uk**
- eOffice | **www.eoffice.net**

When holding meetings, consider hiring professional meeting space. Many offer serviced addresses and secretarial services too, so there could be great continuity for your clients if they only have to remember one location. Probably the largest serviced office provider in the UK is Regus. You can access 15 days use of Regus offices as part of the Enterprise Nation member package.

Make the most of the email marketing opportunity every time you click 'send'. Include a professional email signature or sign-off that has your basic contact details (name, company, postal address, telephone, etc.) and also maybe mention any seasonal or product offers. Indeed, you are required by law, following the introduction of the Companies Act 2006, to display the company's registered office address on your website and any electronic communications.

# On the phone

When running a business from home, consider who will be picking up the phone! It's cheap and sometimes free to get an 0845 local rate number or an 0870 national rate number for your business. This will hide where you're based and divert your calls to wherever you specify. But beware: sometimes having such a number – especially with national rates – might put customers off ringing you.

If you use a landline number it's best to have a separate line for your home and your business. It will stop your business calls from being answered by the kids and also give you a chance to escape work calls when you want to. And these days you don't need to invest in an actual second line. I use a VoIP (voice over internet protocol) phone, which uses my broadband connection to make and receive calls.

Another idea is to get some help from a call-handling service. They will answer your calls with your company name, text urgent messages to you and email the others, giving you a big business feel for about £50 per month. We use a service called Moneypenny, but there are other providers too, including Regus and Answer.

- Moneypenny | **www.moneypenny.co.uk**

- Regus | **www.regus.co.uk**

- Answer | **www.answer.co.uk**

You might consider a 'follow-me number' to ensure you're available when you need to be and able to deliver the right impression to clients. This involves choosing a number and directing calls from it to your landline or mobile. The beauty is that you have the option to select either a freephone or a geographical number so, say you'd like to have a Manchester area code, simply buy a number starting with 0161. The same goes for hundreds of other locations.

Route calls to your mobile and choose a local number in any of 21 countries to have a virtual local presence with Skype (**www.skype.com**). Offer virtual phone numbers where the caller pays a local rate, regardless of where you are, through Vonage (**www.vonage.co.uk**) or direct calls to you from a chosen number using internet technology and a virtual receptionist at eReceptionist (**www.ereceptionist.co.uk**).

# PROTECT THE BRAND

In the last chapter you registered with HM Revenue & Customs and possibly Companies House. Now you need to consider your intellectual property.

You may decide to register a trademark to protect your company name or brand or, if you've come up with a unique invention, a patent. This means that companies can't come along and use your name or invention without your permission.

## The four forms of IP

There are four different kinds of intellectual property that you can protect.

### 1. PATENTS

Patents are, essentially, what makes things work. For example, says the Intellectual Property Office (IPO), "what makes a wheel turn or the chemical formula of your favourite fizzy drink".

### 2. TRADEMARKS

These are "signs (like words and logos) that distinguish goods and services in the marketplace".

### 3. DESIGNS

What a logo or product looks like, "from the shape of an aeroplane to a fashion item".

### 4. COPYRIGHT

An automatic right that comes into existence for anything written or recorded.

Visit the UK Intellectual Property Office website (**www.ipo.gov.uk**) to carry out searches, register trademarks and read up on all things IP-related.

# IP Q&A

We asked Cally Robson from She's Ingenious (**www.shesingenious.org**), The Association for Women with New Product Ideas and Inventions, for her advice about getting your products registered and protected by the Intellectual Property Office:

**Q.** *Is IP protection as important whether you're delivering products or services? i.e. whether I'm selling a homemade pot or design concepts, should I still consider protection?*

"Yes. Whatever the nature of your business, to distinguish yourself from the competition you need to be unique in some way. IP law basically offers a way to protect what is special about your business. Although IP might feel less relevant in a service-oriented business, it is just as key. Registering a distinct logo and/or name as a trademark, buying a strong web address, and building your brand should all be part of the IP strategy for a service-based business."

**Q.** *How much will it cost to protect my idea or design?*

"Although they look cheap to register, patents can be expensive to maintain, running into hundreds of thousands of pounds if you want to take your concept worldwide. So they tend to suit ideas that have big market potential.

"By contrast, registered designs might cost just a few hundred pounds. But they are a weaker form of protection – they can't block someone else from tweaking your design and taking the same basic concept to market.

"Registering your own trademark costs just a couple of hundred pounds, although this cost can vary depending on what territories you intend to register your trademark – whether just the UK, Europe or worldwide.

"The IPO website has a basic confidentiality agreement you can download for free and amend to suit your specific needs, to protect your ideas in discussions."

Q. *At what stage in the business set-up should I seek protection?*

"Right at the start you should learn about the different forms of IP and how protection works. The insights you gain could drastically affect how you shape your business and its future ability to be distinctive, block competitors, scale up, and command pricing that will earn you profits."

Q. *Would you recommend taking advice via the IPO website or commissioning an IP expert?*

"Definitely learn the basics from the IPO website first, and also The British Library's Business and IP Centre in London (**www.bl.uk/bipc**). Make use of the free first sessions provided by IP experts to ask detailed questions. But always, always before you commission an IP expert, absorb as much as you can from the experience of seasoned entrepreneurs and inventors. Understanding the subtleties of how IP protection actually works in business is essential if you want to grow a sustainable, thriving enterprise."

# Chapter Five

## TECH SET-UP AND THE
## PERFECT WORK
## ENVIRONMENT

ONE OF THE GREAT benefits of being your own boss is the ability to work where and how you like, whilst wearing what you like!

Create an environment to suit you and equip your office with all the technology, tools and accessories that will deliver a productive end result.

# YOUR TECH SET-UP

Building the right IT system for your business needn't mean starting from scratch or spending lots of money. Once your business grows you can upgrade your technology as and when funds become available. To start with, there are affordable, even free, solutions that can get you up and running in no time at all. If you've decided to buy a new computer, here are the things to look out for:

## PROCESSOR

The processor is the speed of your computer. The higher the number, the faster your computer can run.

## MEMORY

More memory (RAM) means faster overall performance and enables your computer to run more programs at once. Try and buy a computer with as much RAM as you can afford. A common frustration amongst computer users is how long it can take to launch programs and switch between them. More RAM equals less waiting.

## HARD DRIVE

The hard drive gives you space for all your data and programs. This can easily be expanded with a second, external hard drive, but you'll be surprised at how quickly it will fill up, especially if you're storing designs and images on your computer.

## MULTIFUNCTION PRINTER

Even though I find myself using it less these days, with most information passed around electronically, I still think it's too early to pronounce the printer dead, especially if you use a multifunction printer like I do.

It's a real space-saver – imagine keeping a printer, scanner, photocopier and fax machine in one office! You'd have no room to do any work. Mine sits neatly on my desk and is particularly handy when I want to email sketches to my designer. He uses his to archive printed documents. When he receives important letters, for example, he scans them into his computer and recycles the hard copy! We're both on our way to paperless home offices.

## EXTERNAL HARD DRIVE

I've already mentioned external hard drives. They're great for extending the storage capacity of your computer – so you can keep more data and programs – but they're especially useful for backing up the entirety of your machine. This is a vital process which you should do regularly – imagine the implications if your computer crashed and wouldn't reboot; or if something worse happened. Look for ones with USB 2.0 connections or, if you're using a Mac, a relevant FireWire or Thunderbolt connection.

They're easy to set up – you just plug them in and they show up in your operating system as another drive. You can then just drag and drop important folders or use special software that automates the process for you. Macs have this software built-in, as do the latest PCs. If your machine is without, try SuperDuper! for the Mac and True Image for the PC.

- SuperDuper! | **www.shirt-pocket.com/SuperDuper**
- True Image | **www.acronis.com**

## VOIP PHONES

You can make serious savings on your phone bill by using a VoIP phone. VoIP stands for voice over internet protocol and it basically means making calls over the internet rather than by using your phone line. As such, it's a much cheaper way of making calls (it's sometimes free). And it's the easiest way to set up a second phone line. The VoIP phone I use is made by a company called IPEVO (**www.ipevo.com**).

## OFFICE SOFTWARE

By far the industry standard in office software is, of course, Microsoft Office, which includes a word processor as well as presentation and spreadsheet program.

- Microsoft Office for small business | **office.microsoft.com/en-gb/small-business**

If you're trying to bootstrap, try free alternative OpenOffice. It does pretty much everything that Microsoft Office can do, plus it can open and save Microsoft Office files too. It does take some getting used to, but the support is pretty good. It's worth a try!

- OpenOffice | **www.openoffice.org**

# Getting connected

You'll need broadband right from the start: during your research, while you're setting up your business, through to when it grows and takes over the world!

Your two main options are ADSL broadband, which is offered by companies like BT and Sky, and cable broadband from Virgin Media. The biggest difference is that ADSL requires a phone line, while cable broadband does not.

The advantage of cable broadband is that if you don't have a landline phone, and always use your mobile, you can save money by not having to pay line rental on your phone as well as on your internet connection. It's often faster, too, but you'll need to check whether it's available in your area. ADSL broadband is more commonplace and there are lots of companies offering it.

As always, read the fine print before you sign anything. Here are some things to look out for:

## PRICE

Some broadband prices seem really cheap but often the prices advertised are for the first few months of an 18-month contract, so make sure you know what you're getting into before you sign anything.

## USAGE

Some broadband companies will set restrictions on the amount of data you can download in a month and sometimes even charge you extra if you go over your agreed limit. These limits rarely affect most users, but if your business is the kind that needs to send and receive lots of information, look for deals with generous monthly download allowances. Or, better still, unlimited downloads.

## CUSTOMER SUPPORT

If you're installing broadband for the first time, you might need some help setting up and also, once you're up and running, knowing what to do when your connection suddenly drops. For these sorts of queries it's handy to have good customer support, so check to see what's on offer and, crucially, how much it would cost to call for help.

## NETWORK

Setting up a network used to be the work of professionals and, I suppose, in big companies it still is. But setting up a network for your home by yourself is much easier these days. Your internet service provider may have already provided you with a router – a device that allows you to share your internet connection with other computers in your home. And many are now giving out wireless routers for free, so you can connect to the internet all around the house – and even in the garden!

There are two types of wireless router: one for ADSL and another for cable internet. Check with your internet service provider to find out which is the best router for your type of connection.

I didn't get a free wireless router with my provider, but a friend recommended one that I can to you too. It's from a company called Netgear (**www.netgear.co.uk**), and it looks quite nice too!

# Email

All computers come with email software preinstalled. On PCs the software is called Outlook Express (or on newer PCs Windows Mail) and on Macs it's just called Mail. If you've got Microsoft Office you might use Outlook (or Entourage, as it's called in the Mac version), which is Outlook Express's big sister. It includes calendar and address book features.

## POP MAIL VS. WEB MAIL

There are two kinds of email – POP and IMAP. Non-web-based email that you usually use in a program like Outlook or Apple's Mail is called POP mail and it works by downloading messages from a server onto your computer. But IMAP is becoming more popular, as it is more convenient for those who use email on several devices, like a laptop, a home computer or a smartphone. You can get POP on those things too, but you end up with copies of messages, which can be confusing. IMAP does a better job of keeping everything in sync, so your inbox looks the same wherever you are.

Web mail is accessed through a web browser, like Google Chrome or Internet Explorer. However, whilst that's very handy and such web mail is widely provided for free through services like Microsoft's Hotmail or Google's Gmail, it is perhaps less professional-sounding than POP mail. POP mail can be addressed at your domain (for example, *emma@enterprisenation.com*). My Hotmail address, on the other hand, is *enterprisenation@hotmail.co.uk*, which doesn't look quite as good!

But there is a solution that Google provides. It's called Google Apps (**www.google.com/a**) and it allows you to use all of its web-based features, like email, calendar and instant messaging at your own address. It's especially good for small businesses and organisations – and it's free! You just need to own your own domain, like I do: **www.enterprisenation.com**

## INSTANT MESSAGING

A great way to stay in touch with friends and colleagues is by instant messaging (IM), which allows you to exchange typed messages over the internet in real-time. So it's not like email, where there's typically a delay in the response. Instant messaging is more like chatting. And if you work from home, it instils an office-like atmosphere in your very own home office.

Lots of instant messaging programs also allow you to make video and voice calls. The program I use is Skype (**www.skype.com**) and it integrates text, voice and video chat. It allows me to make free calls to other Skype users and to landline or mobile phones for a small fee, which is deducted from pay-as-you-go style 'Skype credit'.

You can even assign a landline-sounding phone number to your Skype account, so you can receive calls at your computer, using a VoIP handset, or divert calls to your mobile when you're out and about. It's worth trying it out before you spend money installing a second line.

# Support

If you're in need of assistance with anything from hardware set-up to software installation, then call in the help of a local IT expert. You may know a neighbour who's a dab hand at technology. If not, check out one of a growing number of companies who send a 'geek' direct to your door, or visit our site to gain access to a whole range of friendly technical experts.

- Geeks-on-Wheels | **www.geeks-on-wheels.com**
- The TechGuys | **www.thetechguys.com**
- Geek Squad | **www.geeksquad.co.uk**
- Tech Tuesday on Enterprise Nation | **www.enterprisenation.com**
- HP Business Answers group on LinkedIn | **www.linkedin.com/groups/HP-Business-Answers-3692681**
- *50 Top Tech Tools and Tips* by David Sandy | **www.enterprisenation.com/shop/50toptechtoolsandtips**

# 10 free cloud apps for your business

Cloud apps are not only fantastically useful, they also don't take up room on your computer and you don't have to worry about backing up your data. To top it off, they're, more often than not, free to use.

Here are ten of our favourite free cloud apps for business . . .

1   Dropbox (**www.dropbox.com**) | Dropbox is like a thumb drive in the sky. It's a folder that sits on your computer, but its contents are stored remotely and synced across other computers and devices that are signed into your Dropbox account. No-nonsense sharing, if you're working with others, and peace of mind that all your work is backed up.

2   Evernote (**www.evernote.com**) | Evernote is a bit like Dropbox, but for your brain. It helps you "remember everything" by allowing you to capture notes and ideas, photos and screen grabs, sounds and links, sync them automatically to the cloud and access them from practically anywhere – great for the planning stages of your business, or for when ideas strike you on the go.

3   Google Docs (**docs.google.com**) | As broadband gets quicker and more reliable, Google Docs is becoming a bit of a threat to Microsoft Office. It includes apps for word processing, spreadsheets, presentations, drawings and forms – except all the apps run inside your browser rather than on your desktop. All of your work is stored in the cloud and it's super easy to collaborate with others in *real time* on the same document.

4   Gmail and Google Calendar (**mail.google.com, calendar.google.com**) | I've mentioned Gmail before, but did you know Google also make excellent calendar software? Both are really useful if you plan to work on the move.

5   Google Analytics (**www.google.com/analytics**) | When your website is up and running, you'll want to know how many people are visiting. Google Analytics, like most of Google's services, is free, and helps you understand your website statistics, including where your visitors are from, which pages they visited the most, and how they found your website in the first place.

**6** HootSuite (**www.hootsuite.com**) | If social media is part of your marketing plan – and it probably is! – there's no better way to manage your social media presence than with HootSuite. It keeps you on top of your Twitter, Facebook and LinkedIn accounts, as well as what your customers and potential customers are saying about your business.

**7** Delicious (**www.delicious.com**) | Delicious is a bookmarking service that keeps all of your important links in the cloud so you can get to them from any computer.

**8** Toodledo (**www.toodledo.com**) | There's so much to do when starting a business, but you can keep on top of all your tasks with this free app. Get tasks out of your inbox by forwarding them to your Toodledo email address, organise them by folders, tags, context and subtasks, and sync them with your smartphone.

**9** Basecamp (**www.basecamp.com**) | If some tasks involve other people and form part of larger projects, check out project management software, Basecamp. It allows you to share files, deliver projects on time and keep communication organised and out of your inbox.

**10** MailChimp (**www.mailchimp.com**) | To make sure your business message is in other people's inboxes, put together a newsletter with MailChimp, send it out to your customer mailing list and track its success. Just make sure people have signed up to your mailing list before hitting 'send'!

# YOUR PERFECT WORK ENVIRONMENT

Create the perfect work environment for you and your business and follow this checklist to ensure you're working profitably and productively.

## FIND DEDICATED SPACE

As your business is likely to be based at home, try to create an area in the house that functions as your dedicated workspace. That way you can mentally adjust yourself to be in business mode when in that space. It helps you to know when you should be working and when you should be taking a break.

It will also help make it clear to friends and family that when you're in your home office or studio, you're working. And when the door's closed, it means, 'I'm busy. Please don't disturb'.

This dedicated space could be a spare room, in the attic, under the stairs or even the garden shed.

## A LIGHT TOUCH

Lots of light is good for your mood and work pace but avoid too much task-light shining on the computer monitor. As for colours on the walls, go for light shades as they will make the space look bigger, and consider mirrors to bounce light around.

## INVEST IN A GOOD DESK AND CHAIR

Depending on the nature of your business, you could be spending a good few hours each day at the desk and in your chair, so be sure they're both sturdy and comfortable! Buy a chair that's designed for computer use – and try it out first. Sitting in an awkward position can put your body under stress, so make sure you can adjust the chair's height and angle to suit you. Ideally, your feet should be flat on the floor and your back straight. Getting this right will make working from home so much more comfortable!

Get a good, sturdy desk that can accommodate your computer, monitor, keyboard and mouse. The top of your monitor should be at eye level and the monitor itself about an arm's length away from you.

## DOUBLE-UP

Invest in storage boxes and turn your wardrobes into filing cabinets! Or buy big boxes, label them well and then find a place to hide them away; maybe doubling up as a chair for visitors.

## A SPRING CLEAN

Wondering what to do with all the stuff in the room that you want to use as your home office? Take space with a company like Access Storage and have your goods accessible but out of the way, or give them up to a recycling company such as London Re-use or Freecycle, so your unwanted items can go to a home that does want them!

- Access Self Storage | **www.accessstorage.com**

- London Re-use | **www.londonreusecommercial.org**

- Freecycle | **www.freecycle.org**

## VISION BOARD

Set goals and stay on track with the use of a vision board.

A vision board is a visual reminder of what you're trying to achieve in your business and personal life and, attached to the home office wall, can act as a useful daily prompt and pep talk!

Buy a basic board and stick to it pictures that represent your ambitions; places you want to visit, targets for the company, and people with whom you enjoy spending time. Glance at it each day to remind yourself of everything you're working for and towards and to measure how the business is doing. Such a board will encourage you to stay motivated and hit the targets you've set as well as maintaining the bigger picture of where you want the business to go.

In Chapter Thirteen we look at ways to grow the business without outgrowing the home so you can successfully increase turnover whilst still benefiting from the upsides of working from home; that's not a bad vision to have!

## INSPIRATION WALL

An inspiration wall is similar to the above, although as a creative business it's a great idea to create an inspiration wall or board in your workspace. Pin things up that will get the creative juices flowing – postcards, fabrics, photos, magazine clippings etc. You can add to it or change it regularly to ensure your work doesn't become stale.

# Chapter Six
## STARTING ON A
## BUDGET

# BOOT-STRAPPING TO BEGIN WITH

YOU PROBABLY ALREADY have much of what you need to get started – a computer, mobile phone, some craft tools – so you might not need to buy much more equipment depending on your business. Here are some tips for keeping initial costs low.

## Start the business from home

Why take on the cost of an office when your spare room/attic/garden shed will do just as well? Think of the money you'll save: no premises, no commute, no overpriced sandwiches at lunchtime . . . ! We've already talked about the admin side of starting from home along with information on how to turn a home office into the perfect working environment. Plus if you have children, you can work the business around them so that you get the most out of your time together – not to mention the savings on childcare!

*This is what Michelle Grey decided to do when she started her home interiors business after becoming a mum . . .*

# BEAUTIFUL BUSINESS:
# LUXURY INTERIORS & KOOL KIDS ROOMS

**Name:** Michelle Grey

**Business:** Luxury Interiors & Kool Kids Rooms

**Website:** www.koolkidsrooms.co.uk | www.luxuryinteriors.co.uk

**Social media:** @koolkidsrooms | www.facebook.com/koolkidsrooms

Michelle Grey first came up with the idea for her interior accessories business back in 2011 after the birth of her twin girls.

> "Prior to becoming a mum, I had worked in finance in the computer industry, but due to the cost of childcare I decided not to return to work. I had always aspired to work for myself in some capacity within the interiors industry."

For the first six months after her twins were born life was hectic, as Michelle got to grips with being a first-time mum. However, not one for sitting still, she enrolled on a college course to learn how to professionally sew soft furnishings.

> "After the first year I passed the exam and decided this was what I wanted to pursue. It was a gradual process during my second year that I came up with the name Luxury Interiors, and my business was born!"

Luxury Interior's first customers came through word of mouth from friends and family. After that, Michelle began to build up her practical experience and her photo portfolio. From there, she had some leaflets printed and delivered around her local area.

> "I also started off with an advert in my local *Yellow Pages* which helped me gain customers outside of my initial circle."

Michelle initially promoted the business through the *Yellow Pages*, *Thomson Directory* and printed leaflets, but in 2006 she realised that this might not be the best method anymore.

"I embarked on a sharp learning curve of building an online presence and paid a local company to build me a four-page website. I knew absolutely nothing about websites back then but I had to learn fast. When I compare the first version that went live with what I have today, they are miles apart!"

Since creating the website, Michelle has also set up social media accounts and keeps her customers up-to-date about new products and developments that way too.

Keen to grow the business even further, in 2009 Michelle decided she wanted to set up an e-commerce site selling curtain poles, tracks, blinds, tiebacks, and so on, called Luxury Curtain Poles.

"Initially I thought it would be easy to do – this time I understood my current website and had continued to develop it. I worked with a local company designing what I wanted and I set about adding hundreds of products, prices, descriptions and images. It was nine months of hard work alongside my Luxury Interiors business and looking after my family. What I came to understand was that an e-commerce website is a totally different animal to just an information based website."

After a year, Michelle decided that she didn't want to pursue this any further. However, she had been developing ideas about children's bedding and accessories as well.

"In the summer of 2011, I made contact with a supplier of children's bedding and curtains and soon Kool Kids Rooms was born! I initially started developing the business and selling the range on my Luxury Curtain Poles website, but it was obvious that if I was serious about creating a brand I had to move the business to its own domain name."

In 2012, Michelle did just that and the Kool Kids Rooms website was re-launched on its own domain and with a new branding concept.

"It has continued to go from strength to strength and I am really excited about 2013."

For Michelle, 2013 is looking very exciting. Although she doesn't currently export her items, she does receive a number of enquiries to ship items abroad, especially to the large community of British expats.

"Currently this isn't something I'm set up to do, but I have already had initial discussions with a few courier companies and in 2013 I intend to start to work with one that I trust and expand into Europe and beyond."

Alongside this, Michelle wants to continue to grow in the UK and expand her product lines.

"I would love to recruit an extra pair of hands as I currently do everything and sometimes it does just get a bit too much! All this is run alongside my very first business Luxury Interiors, which is now ten years old, so I must be doing something right!"

# Top tip!

"Identify your weaknesses and try to find good people you trust to plug those gaps. If you struggle with technology, find a small business you can work with that can look after this, or if you have no idea how to design an advert or leaflets find someone that can!"

# Online shops

If you are thinking about setting up an online shop to curate a range of products for the home from other suppliers, it is worth noting that there are other costs to consider.

Initially, you will need capital to buy in stock, and you'll also need to decide whether you want to buy this stock outright or on sale or return.

The Prince's Trust can give you more information on which option might be best for you: **tinyurl.com/saleorreturn**

Another factor to consider is where you will be sourcing your products. A good idea is to visit large trade fairs such as Top Drawer in London or the Spring and Autumn Fairs in Birmingham. These events are for trade only, so you must be able to demonstrate your trading credentials. Even if you have not launched your business yet, you can still attend – just as long as you can provide some kind of proof of intent for your new business (such as a website in progress). It is always worth talking to the organisers. Once you have launched, it is simply a case of registering on the website of the event.

Remember that wholesalers and suppliers often have a minimum order amount, which can be anything from a £50 spend up to £1,000 or more. At the start, it is a good idea to stick with suppliers who offer lower minimum orders to minimise your financial risk and the demands placed on what little storage space you do have.

Another good idea is to visit lots of smaller craft events to discover new talent. You can also research independent sellers online.

If you are planning to sell vintage goods or plan to customise or upcycle these items, where will you source them? Bear in mind bigger markets in cities such as London tend to be much more pricey, so try to find out of town markets and car boot sales where prices will be lower. And don't forget to barter. This will keep your buying and production costs down.

• Top Drawer | **www.topdrawer.co.uk**

• Spring Fair | **www.springfair.com**

## Beg, borrow and barter!

When starting out, access all the resources you can.

Do you need a space in which to hold an event? Approach someone who has the space and would welcome the footfall you can bring. After some heavy duty equipment to make your products that your start-up budget just can't afford? Reach out to someone who has the equipment and ask whether you can use it in their downtime hours. It is perfectly possible to put together a business/event/project through bartering your way to success!

TIP { The beauty of barter

Many start-up businesses barter their goods and services, e.g. "I'll produce a sales brochure for you in exchange for some handmade curtains for my living room." This works well – both parties get what they want. But take heed of the tax implications. Bartering means money doesn't show up in your accounts, but there has been an exchange of goods and services which implies a taxable activity. The taxman could view bartering as a way to avoid tax. Nevertheless, with so many beneficial arrangements underway, maybe it's time they revised the tax situation?

# WORKING 5 TO 9

You can plan the business, register the business and indeed continue to run the business successfully by 'working 5 to 9' – this is the term I apply to the five-million-plus people who are holding down a day job and building a business at night and weekends. While you might work as an estate agent during the day, you could get your pottery business up and running in your spare time, giving you the financial security of your full-time job and allowing you to build the business at your own pace.

Working 5 to 9 is a very sensible way to start and grow – you give yourself the time to build confidence and cash flow in the business, plus you can keep putting money aside until you're ready to go full time. If you're keeping hold of the day job and growing the business in your spare time, here's what you need to do regarding your current job and boss.

## The contract

If you have written terms and conditions of employment they are likely to contain reference to the pursuit of personal business ventures outside your contracted working hours. The clauses to look out for include 'the employee's duties and obligations' and what is commonly known as 'whole time and effort'. These clauses usually require the employee to devote the whole of their time, attention and abilities to the business of the employer.

If your contract contains these or similar clauses, don't despair, as it doesn't necessarily mean you can't pursue your business. Many employment contracts are drafted using standard templates with little consideration to personal circumstance. You know your job better than anyone, so if you don't think your business venture will affect the way you do your job, it probably won't – and your employer will recognise this. Having checked how things stand in the contract, it's time to talk things through with your boss.

## The conversation

Treat it as an amicable and informal conversation to gauge your employer's initial reaction.

I asked Patrick Lockton, a qualified lawyer and head of Matrix Law Group, for his take on the matter and advice on how employees should go about having this conversation:

> "When you approach your employer, be prepared to negotiate, be flexible and compromise. If you think it appropriate, make it clear your business venture will in no shape or form affect your ability to do your job or affect your employer's interests. If anything, it will make you a better, more confident and experienced employee and it will not cost your employer a thing."

Patrick goes on to say:

"After having such a conversation, you can do one of two things:

"1. if your employer has not expressed any concerns about your intentions and you have no concerns of your own, disclose your intentions to your employer anyway. Treat it as something you want to do for the sake of clarity and for the record, as opposed to something you want their permission for; or

"2. if your employer has expressed concerns, try and negotiate a package that you are both happy with. Address their concerns, agree some ground rules and get their permission in writing. Give your employer as much helpful information as possible. If you are going to need some time off or to change your hours then this is the time to bring it up.

"Always take written notes so that you don't forget what was said and so you can remind your employer what was agreed."

So long as you're not competing with your employer or breaching their trust, you shouldn't have any problem at all in pursuing your 5 to 9 ambitions. After all, as Patrick says, your employer benefits from all the new skills you're picking up, and it doesn't cost them a penny in training or resources!

## TIP { Time management

Managing your time when also working full-time can be difficult but there are things you can do to make sure everything gets done and that your business doesn't interfere with your day job.

Make calls to suppliers before work in the morning and use your lunch hour to answer customer emails, or visit a potential new stockist, freeing up your evenings and weekends to take care of orders, packing and so on. It can also be a good idea to make clear task lists to make sure you get everything done in the time you have!

*Lou Gardner runs her business The Vintage Twist Company alongside her full-time job and has found that it is vital to prioritise her time effectively . . .*

# BEAUTIFUL BUSINESS:
# THE VINTAGE TWIST COMPANY

**Name:** Lou Gardner

**Business:** The Vintage Twist Company

**Website:** www.thevintagetwistcompany.co.uk

**Social media:** www.facebook.com/thevintagetwistcompany |
www.thevintagetwistcompany.blogspot.co.uk

Lou Gardner's idea for her upcycling business, The Vintage Twist Company, came after she had been making gifts for friends and family and wanted to take her idea to the next stage.

> "I sold my first piece on eBay – I'd been selling bits and bobs on there for years so it seemed the obvious place to start. A high percentage of consumers use it to source goods. A lady from London purchased a blanket box I'd redesigned and loved it! She even wrote a testimonial for me as well as leaving positive feedback."

Lou soon realised the huge possibilities with this method of upcycling and how she could turn it into a business.

> "I didn't think that sculptures would be that marketable, but applying the upcycling to furniture and accessories would be more accessible."

As her two favourite pastimes are finding vintage things and shopping, sourcing pieces to work on is very easy!

> "Sometimes I find it difficult to accommodate all the pieces that I find and just have to walk away, but I'm also very lucky that people give me pieces rather than landfill them so it's nice to be doing my bit for the environment too. I once rescued a 1970s vinyl pouffe from a pile of rubbish that had been tipped on the side of the road – it's now revitalised with sunflower fabric and a decadent trim!"

Since selling that first piece on eBay, Lou has been growing the business and working hard to get established.

"I've had pieces in several local shops and used social media to spread the word."

The Vintage Twist Company is still a small 'kitchen table' business, but it has been growing since January 2011, creating chairs, tables, dressing tables, lamps and more.

"Being able to create stylish, unusual and unique pieces mostly out of damaged, ugly, tired items that people have fallen out of love with by transforming them with fabric and paints never ceases to amaze me. But knowing the people who buy them will treasure them is so satisfying – one customer bought a heavy old wooden storage box that I'd transformed into a child's pirate treasure chest complete with a fancy brass key that I sourced for it. He wrote to say he was so pleased with it and it would be kept for a family heirloom!"

However, as with many other small business owners, Lou finds that time can be very short!

"Like many other people in my shoes, I have a day job too, which makes it very difficult to do everything I'd like to. This includes completing my website!"

She has found that it can be difficult to decide how to spend her time most effectively. Because of this she has chosen to use existing sales sites to sell her products before completing her own website.

"Facebook gains awareness and potential sales but there's a fine line between potential customers and people who just 'like' what you do, or of course copy your work. I've found that both eBay and Etsy have huge audiences but they work in different ways – for example, eBay customers are often particularly looking for a bargain whereas Etsy is more of a handmade site where people expect to pay more."

The Vintage Twist Company has big plans for the next 12 months.

"I'd like to find a balance between being a designer/maker and all the administrative jobs. I have limitless ideas on redesigning furniture and accessories as well as sales and marketing strategies but the latter seems to require the most amount of time! After all, there's no point in making the product if I can't sell it."

Lou is also starting a degree in Retail Interior Design in April 2013 to add to her diploma in Interior Design, and is hoping that she will be able to grow the business by approaching interior designers and shops to stock her products, as well as spending more time on advertising to get the word about The Vintage Twist Company out there!

# Top tip!

"Be prepared to work hard, don't give up, listen to advice and take what you need. Don't forget to take a rest and enjoy what you do!"

# Chapter Seven
# MONEY
# MANAGEMENT

IT'S BECOME SO much easier to start a business on a budget and keep finances in check by keeping overheads low. This chapter shows how to manage your finances, as well as offering a simple way to calculate profit through use of a basic spreadsheet.

# STRAIGHTFORWARD FINANCE

When running a business you'll want to be sure earnings are higher than outgoings.

Earnings are also referred to as revenue, turnover or income and this should be a greater figure than outgoings, overheads or costs. Let's look at the items that come within each category.

## INCOMING

Earn from selling your product or service and any associated income opportunities. For example, you set up a business selling unique handmade cushions. From the outset, earn income from:

- selling 24 x handmade cushions at £25 per cushion = £600 income per week

- speaking at events to teach others how to make cushions = £150 per event

- custom requests, e.g. a unique and one-off production = £75 per item

- developing a blog on the topic of cushions that attracts cushion-istas as readers and paying advertisers as your secondary customers – £priceless!

OUTGOING

Here are the costs; some payable at start-up stage and others ongoing:

- **Salary** – how much do you need to pay yourself? (You will be pleasantly surprised at how thriftily you can live when not commuting.)

- **Property** – start the business from home and avoid the cost of a pricey second office.

- **Raw materials and equipment** – what are the materials you need to deliver and promote your finished cushions? And do you need any equipment to make that product; a sewing machine, computer, printer, smartphone or camera?

- **Insurance** – be insured from the start and choose a policy that covers all your needs.

- **Website/promotion materials** – we will cover on later how you can build a home on the web and promote the business on a shoestring of a budget.


# Cash flow

Managing cash flow is crucial for the survival of the business, so in order to stay on top of this, keep records of all incomings and outgoings in a basic spreadsheet.

On the following page is an example spreadsheet you can use.

Keeping records up to date and being on top of invoices means you'll have positive cash flow and be in a position to buy the stock and supplies needed to make the business function.

The most common reasons for a disruption to cash flow are customers that don't pay, not selling enough products or having too many outgoings. So what can you do to avoid this?

| INCOMING | |
|---|---:|
| Product sales | £xx |
| Sponsorship/Advertising | £xx |
| Other contracts | £xx |
| | |

| OUTGOINGS | |
|---|---:|
| Salary | (£xx) |
| IT | (£xx) |
| Office | (£xx) |
| Raw materials/equipment | (£xx) |
| Insurance | (£xx) |
| Marketing & promotion | (£xx) |
| Other | (£xx) |
| | |

| PROFIT | £XX |
|---|---:|

## STAY ON TOP OF YOUR CASH FLOW

Try to do your cash flow budget regularly so that you always have a clear idea about where your business stands.

- Save costs where possible – you will need to spend some money to get the business up and running but try to keep these to a minimum so outgoings don't start to rack up.

- Have customers pay before you ship their items.

- Plan effectively – if you know there is a craft fair coming up that you want to attend but it might eat into your budget, start planning for this a couple of months early. When the time comes, it won't be such a big outgoing expense.

## INVOICES

Be on time with invoicing and keep a record of amounts outstanding. I have a simple spreadsheet with five columns labelled 'client', 'invoice amount', 'invoice number', 'date submitted' and 'date paid'.

Your invoices should be a simple document with basic but thorough details. The less cause for question on the invoice, the faster it will be paid!

Settle invoices as promptly as you can but make use of the credit extended to you. Your suppliers will be grateful and should repay you with good service.

You can balance the budget with a piece of accounting software. Priced at between £50 and £100 for 'starter' versions, these packages offer sales and expense tracking, invoice templates, bank reconciliations and basic bookkeeping.

## RECEIPTS

Keep business-related receipts in a place where they're easy to find. I have a big wicker box that doubles as a collecting place for receipts. It's helpful that they're all in one place when it's time to do the VAT return.

# PRICING PRODUCTS

When pricing items you don't want to be pricing too high and putting off customers. Nor, however, do you want to price too low and end up not making any money!

There isn't one simple solution for pricing your products. Many designers and crafters will approach this differently. What's key, though, is to account for the *time* you take to produce each item; factor this in and price competitively against what others are charging in the market.

Let's take the example of making a bespoke throw and look at how you would work out a price . . .

## THROWING TOGETHER A PRICE

The cost for materials needed to make your throw – including fabric, thread, company labels, zips/buttons and embellishments – comes to £3. When deciding how much your materials cost, you don't need to take into account the total price of the supply if you've only used a fraction of it. For example, you were able to buy the fabric for the throws at £5 per five metres, but you've only used a metre per throw. The estimated cost for the fabric per handbag should therefore be £1.

You then need to add the cost of your time – say it takes one hour for you to make each throw and you think that your hourly rate is roughly £7.

Now that you have the base cost for your product (£3 for all the materials plus £7 for labour, making £10 in total), you need to decide how much you want to mark it up in order to sell to customers.

Many businesses use the 2.5 *formula*, whereby they multiply base cost by 2.5 and use that as their price. In our example this would make the throw £25.

Once you have that figure, you need to look at your competitors in more detail – are they offering anything similar, and are their products of a similar quality, size, style etc.? Depending on the results of this research, you may want to revise your price, either increasing it if you think your product is worth more, or decreasing it to make it more competitive.

Over time, you may decide you are producing superior items or sourcing more unique materials so an increase in prices makes sense. Don't be afraid to do this if people recognise they are buying a unique handmade product that justifies it. They'll often be willing to pay a little extra.

# BEAUTIFUL BUSINESS: COO & CO

**Name:** Jenny McCabe

**Business:** Coo & Co

**Website: www.cooandco.co.uk**

Jenny McCabe's handprinted and handmade textiles business Coo & Co was born out of her passion as an artist and her desire to make things people could enjoy and use.

"The mission behind the business is to use natural and, where possible, recycled and up-cycled materials to make useful and stylish items."

Jenny began developing ideas for her business in 2009 and spent the next two years honing her technical skills in screen-printing. In November 2011, Coo & Co was born and Jenny began selling the pieces made in her studio near the Lake District.

"I initially started using Etsy and Folksy, plus blogging on Blogspot. Very quickly the things I listed sold. It gave me the confidence to develop more and then go on to set up my own website."

From there, Jenny moved on to using Facebook, Twitter, Pinterest and her own blog to promote the business, as well as having her work in gallery shops where people will see her pieces and spread the word about what she is doing.

This way, Jenny is growing the business steadily and is finding more and more stockists who want her products.

"I am also doing my first trade fair this year – The British Craft Trade Fair in Harrogate. I am hoping that this will expand the awareness of my brand and get me larger wholesale orders."

Since launching Coo & Co, Jenny has worked alone, but as the business grows, she is looking to outsource some work.

"My plan is to outsource some of the basic sewing next spring once I have the large wholesale orders from the craft fair."

From there, Jenny has set her sights on the rest of the world.

"I would love to go global! I currently sell lots of items through my online shops all over the world, but at the moment I can only take UK wholesale orders. Give me six months and I'll start taking over the world!"

The next year will see Coo & Co growing more and more. Jenny has written a book called *Handprint and Make Your Own Bags*, which is published in March 2013, as well as attending craft fairs and continuing to sell online and through gallery shops.

# Top tips!

Jenny has a number of tips for anyone looking to start a handmade textile business:

1. "You may need some capital to make it easier, otherwise you may struggle with your cash flow.

2. "Work very hard! If you make great things, the exposure will come.

3. "Use social media wisely – be interesting and accessible rather than pushy and repetitive."

4. "Be yourself and have confidence in your products.

5. "Have good friends who will listen to you whinge!"

# SOURCING SUPPLIES AND EQUIPMENT

As with most aspects of the business, research is key! Search for cost-effective and reliable suppliers via the internet or by asking around for personal recommendations.

For example, if you want to start a curtain-making business, you could search online for supplies and find companies such as:

- Merrick & Day | **www.merrick-day.com**
- Colly Brook | **www.collybrook.co.uk**
- Terry's Fabrics | **www.terrysfabrics.co.uk**

Or if you want to make handmade paper decorations, you can find stationery suppliers, such as:

- The Handcrafted Card Company | **www.thehandcraftedcardcompany.co.uk**
- Kooky Kards | **www.kookykards.com**
- Paper Crafter | **www.papercrafter.co.uk**

These are just a selection of what can be found doing a quick search. Online sales sites can also be a great place to source materials. Check out the following websites:

- Etsy | **www.etsy.com**
- eBay | **www.eBay.co.uk**
- Alibaba.com | **www.alibaba.co.uk**

When looking at sourcing supplies, think about how much you're going to use. Even though it's generally more cost-effective, you don't want to interrupt cash flow by buying too much in terms of material and then not receiving the money in from sales, especially if your product has a longer lead time. If buying in smaller quantities, be confident you can get extra supplies quickly if necessary so customers aren't kept waiting!

When it comes to sourcing equipment, if you can't afford to buy new machinery or tools, don't rule out buying second-hand – auction sites and recycling website are useful places to look. Talk to other artisans and crafters as they may be up for sharing tools or upgrading to new equipment and looking for an opportunity to pass on their tools, meaning you get sound equipment at a reduced price.

# BEAUTIFUL BUSINESS:
# BILLY LLOYD CERAMICS

**Name:** Billy Lloyd

**Business:** Billy Lloyd Ceramics

**Website:** www.billylloyd.co.uk

**Social media:** www.facebook.com/billylloydceramics | @billylloydesign

Potter Billy Lloyd knew from a young age that he wanted to work within the creative sector when he was older.

> "I was fortunate to attend a school with a competent ceramics department, which introduced me to the virtues of working with clay at the age of 13. This led to an Art Foundation course in Oxfordshire and a BA (Hons) Ceramics at Camberwell College of Art and Design, London. Upon graduation, I immediately went on to assist Lisa Hammond at Maze Hill Pottery, Greenwich, for one year."

In 2007, Billy formally registered his business and in the same year began a four-year apprenticeship with leading potter and writer Julian Stair.

> "My business was essentially born of an innate desire to design and make objects that serve a functional purpose; objects that I want to use."

He soon found that taking part in open studios and other small exhibitions meant he was introduced to a number of collectors, curators and retailers.

> "The modern aesthetic and functional nature of my ceramics seemed to appeal to a broad demographic and my profile quickly developed – the first retailer to stock my work was Priscilla Carluccio, sister of Sir Terence Conran, whom I met at Julian Stair's studio. Priscilla saw my Stacking Mugs and placed a small order for her shop Few and Far in Knightsbridge. The mugs proved to be popular and as my collection grew so did Priscilla's interest and further orders were placed."

93

Billy believes an online presence is essential and that the rise of social media has made publicity easy, direct and affordable.

> "Twitter, Facebook and Instagram are useful tools of communication, which allow me to build relationships with an array of like-minded individuals and companies. I use them to promote all aspects of my business from the designing and making to exhibiting and selling."

Billy feels that photography is a very evocative means of depicting the different processes of his work and help to illustrate the story of his life as a craftsman. That's something customers are becoming increasingly interested in.

From the start, Billy's business has grown organically through taking part in exhibitions or supplying retailers. This has exposed his work to a wider audience and meant it was often picked up by stylists or journalists, leading to press coverage.

> "This publicity helped to develop my reputation and build new relationships within the craft, design and retail sector. Towards the end of my apprenticeship with Julian Stair in 2011, I won the Cockpit Arts Award, granting me free studio space and business mentoring for one year. The money I saved not having to pay rent meant that I could invest in the tools, equipment and materials that were necessary to establish my first independent studio. In order to grow efficiently, it is important to know in which direction you want to your business to travel so you are appropriately positioned."

Although Billy predominately works alone, he has employed studio assistance in the past to help with certain aspects of making or administration during particularly busy periods. He has also found that collaborations with other designers or retailers have opened up new lines of enquiry (such as an Infusionware range he has developed with London-based tea brokers Lalani and Company) and need consistent communication to mature.

> "Equally, as one of the 65 craft-based businesses at Cockpit Arts in Deptford and a team of staff dedicated to business development to call on, I am never far from good company."

Billy's pieces are sold around the world, with Fennica in Tokyo, which is part of BEAMS Department Store, currently stocking a collection of tableware.

> "Although Edmund de Waal has previously made a limited edition of Tea Bowls, I am the first British potter to supply them with a range of ceramics. I do sell work to overseas

collectors and whilst I am keen to find more international outlets I look forward to building on the relationships I already have."

Billy has big plans for 2013:

"Over the course of the next 12 months I am looking forward to developing new work; in particular realising a substantial lighting commission from SE5 Architects whereby I will make approximately 200 porcelain pendants for Springhill, a residential development in Camberwell Grove, south-east London."

He will also be expanding his range of Infusionware with Lalani and Company. On another note, he will be looking to reevaluate and develop the structure of his business and capitalise on its potential within the luxury sector as a participant in Walpole's Crafted mentoring scheme.

# Top tips!

1. "Be ambitious and pro-active – whether it is the amount you set out to achieve in your day, year or career, you should aspire to innovate high standards of attainment, but do be pragmatic.

2. "Learn to be a competent and effective communicator across a variety of mediums and get to know other designers and makers whose work you respect.

3. "It is important to make a concerted effort when displaying your work for exhibition: consider its relation to your work – it should enhance not overwhelm. Most of all, you must remember that ultimately your work should speak for itself."

# 10 finance tips for House Beautiful Home businesses

*Emily Coltman ACA, Chief Accountant to super-straightforward online accounting system FreeAgent* (**www.freeagent.com**) *and author of* Finance for Small Business *offers her ten top financial tips for small businesses . . .*

### 1. CHOOSE YOUR ACCOUNTING SYSTEM WISELY

"It's important for any business to keep their books in order from day one, but for owners of craft businesses this is even more important than usual, as you'll be dealing with stock and you'll need to keep track of how much you have at any one time.

"Choose a good accounting system with the right level of stock control for your business. If you're buying in stock to sell straight on, you'll need a system with light stock control. (In which case, I do urge you to give FreeAgent a try.)

"If you're making products from raw materials, particularly if your business is growing, look for a system with in-depth stock control. I like Brightpearl (**www.brightpearl.com**) for this."

### 2. BE CAREFUL WITH COMMISSION SALES

"You may sell your products to larger organisations such as countywide craft bodies, who then sell on the items to the public. If you're going to do this, make sure the rate of commission they keep on the sales is fair, and that the interim buyer pays you on time. Don't be caught out by big companies who may pay 'low and slow'."

### 3. BEWARE OF VAT REGISTRATION IF YOU SELL TO THE PUBLIC

"If you're selling your goods directly to the public, for example via your own website, don't register for VAT unless and until you have to (see **www.hmrc.gov.uk/vat**), because to the public, VAT just represents an increase on the cost of your product. Other businesses don't mind it so much, as they can generally claim it back."

## 4. SAVE MONEY WHERE YOU CAN

"If your business won't take up much space, start from home and find out whether you can save money by buying large items for your business second-hand. For example, if you want to make pottery, could you find a potter's wheel for sale on eBay or Gumtree, or even pay to use the wheel at your local art college, rather than buy a new one. But choose your cost savings wisely – see point 5."

## 5. CHOOSE SUPPLIERS CAREFULLY

"When you're thinking of how much you should pay for stock, don't just look for the cheapest option. Think also of quality and ease of acquisition. For example, it may be cheaper to buy your handles for your homemade nursery accessories from abroad, but if they break when tugged by a child, that's bad news for your brand and you could lose business. And there could be myriad reasons (stray ash clouds, political upheavals) why your items can't reach you. There may be import tax too, which will push up the total price paid, so choose your suppliers carefully."

## 6. THINK ABOUT HOW MUCH YOU SHOULD BUY IN AT A TIME

"Suppliers may well give a discount if you buy in larger quantities, and you'll save on postage too, but make sure you don't end up with a pile of unsellable stock, which will put a dent in your profit and tie up cash. Your stock might not be perishable, but if you're making bed linen and you buy a large quantity of bright orange material, will bright orange stay in fashion long enough for you to make and sell the sets?"

## 7. WORK OUT YOUR PROFITABLE LINES

"If you sell more than one kind of product it's a good idea to know which lines bring in the most profit. That's where you should look to focus your time.

"To work out how profitable each line is, take your sale price per unit of that item (for example, £10 per *xx*), then subtract how much each unit costs to produce.

"Make sure you include all your costs. For example, if you're making patchwork cushions, think of not only the fabric and thread but also the cushion pad and zip, and don't forget to include your time for cutting out and sewing up. The more intricate the design, the longer this will take. Use a spreadsheet to help you.

"Ideally do this before you set your prices to customers, because it can be very hard to put prices up right away."

## 8. SET YOUR PRICES CAREFULLY FOR HANDMADE GOODS

"How much of a premium can you charge for handmade goods? For example, if you are making bespoke cross-stitch wedding samplers then your customers will expect these to be sewn by hand, and will anticipate paying a premium accordingly. It will take you a long time. But if you're making clothes, these will usually be machine-stitched. That's quicker, and you won't get away with the same premium.

"If you do something that takes time and commands value in the marketplace, make sure you charge for it and let your customers know about it. It's valuable."

## 9. YOUR WEBSITE OR MINE?

"Should you sell through your own website or through sites such as Etsy or Alibaba? In terms of costs, weigh up the price of building your own site (possibly by using a dedicated e-commerce platform such as **www.powa.com**) or having it built by a professional, against the greater pool of customers you'll find through Etsy but will pay fees for. And don't forget that if you go through your own website you'll also have to invest time marketing the site and maintaining it, or pay someone to do that for you.

"Other useful links are:

• "**www.bigcartel.com** – a platform for hosting your independent shop. They offer free or paid-for plans depending on the number of your products, and they don't take any commission on sales.

- "**www.shopify.com** – create your own online store; you can even use your own domain name. Shopify lets you manage orders, take payments and so on. The price plans start from just £19 a month."

## 10. PLAN FOR THE FUTURE

"No matter how small your business is, it's very important to plan and forecast your sales, costs, profit, and cash coming in and out. This isn't just for large businesses. You won't be able to keep everything in your head no matter how small your business is so write it down and record it!"

# FUNDING

If you think you'll need outside funding for your business, there are a few places you can look.

## FRIENDS AND FAMILY

Friends and family are people you can trust – and asking them for money hopefully won't come with strings attached! Do consider having a written agreement, though, that covers the amount borrowed and a payback schedule, so that both parties are fully aware of exactly what has been agreed.

## THE BANK

Ask to speak to a small business advisor at your local banking branch. Take a copy of your business plan with you and be prepared to talk through it – remember, be clear about what your business does and explain how you can make money from it. It may help to run through this with a friend or colleague beforehand so that you feel prepared when you come to meet the advisor at the bank. If you just need a small amount of capital to get started, you might not necessarily need to get a bank loan – look into whether an overdraft may be better for you.

## CREDIT CARDS

Many a business has been started with help from a flexible friend, but you must shop for the best rates. It's a competitive market and the credit card companies are keen for your business. Make sure you are on time with repayments (to avoid penalty interest charges) and aim to pay back the credit as soon as you can and as sales start coming in. This route is suggested based on start-up costs being small and the ability to pay back at speed so avoiding monthly repayments at high interest rates.

TIP { A clear division

It is a good idea to open a business bank account early on so you don't mix up your business and personal finances, which may complicate record keeping. To open a bank account you'll need to provide details of your business, a business plan and a certificate of incorporation for limited companies.

## STARTUP LOANS

If you're aged between 18 and 30, you are eligible to apply for a StartUp Loan from the government. The average loan size is £2,500 and you receive a mentor as well as the money. Apply online at **www.startuploans.co.uk** and you'll be directed to a local loan distribution partner who will assess your business plan.

## GRANTS

There are grants available from a number of sources, including the government, European Union, local authorities and some charitable organisations, such as The Prince's Trust.

- GOV.UK | **www.gov.uk/business-finance-explained**

- National Enterprise Network (with links to your local enterprise agency) | **www.nationalenterprisenetwork.org**

- The Prince's Trust (funds available to help young people start a business) | **www.princes-trust.org.uk**

- J4b Grants (grants, loans and venture capital) | www.j4bgrants.co.uk

## CROWD FUNDING

Crowd funding is becoming an increasingly popular route for start-ups and growing businesses to raise loans or investment. The idea is you borrow (or get donations) from a crowd of peers. There are a number of sites which enable you to do this, including:

- Seedrs | www.seedrs.com

- Kickstarter | www.kickstarter.co.uk

- Crowdcube | www.crowdcube.com

- Indiegogo | www.indiegogo.com

## INVESTORS

Angel investors and venture capitalists can help raise large amounts of start-up funding or development capital for businesses looking to grow. It might be an idea to consider this route further down the line. It doesn't have to be a gruesome experience, though (à la *Dragons' Den*) as there are plenty of funds and investors out there who are eager to invest their money in good ideas. Unlike banks, investors will be looking for equity, i.e. part ownership in your business, in return for the funds.

- Angels Den | www.angelsden.co.uk

- Funding Circle | www.fundingcircle.com

- UK Business Angels Association | www.bbaa.org.uk

TIP { Free funding guide

To access more detail on these forms of funding, download my free guide on 50 ways to find funding for your business at: www.enterprisenation.com

There are stories of people who have raised money from banks, crowd-funding sites and angels, as well as details on grants, loans and even how to go about raising funds on *Dragons' Den*!

# Chapter Eight
## SELL, SELL, SELL!

YOU HAVE YOUR idea. It's supported by research and a plan pointing you in the right direction. You've sorted out all the kit you need to get going. And with the company registered, and admin and finances in shape, it's time to get into business by making some noise and getting sales!

In this section we'll look at how you achieve sales by selling offline and online, via platform sites and then via your own site.

# OFFLINE SALES

Follow these five steps to make offline sales . . .

### 1. MAKE A LIST (CHECK IT TWICE)

Draw on your existing resources, grab your address book and circle the friends, family, colleagues and acquaintances you think might be interested in your products or service. Add to the list with details of local people and businesses.

### 2. PITCH UP

Write to the people on your list and announce your new business venture. Consider this an opportunity to make your pitch, but don't be too pushy. And remember to address each recipient personally. No one likes a group email!

### 3. FOLLOW UP

Follow up in a few days' time, either with another email or, better still, a phone call. Take some soundings as to the success of your pitch and react accordingly. If the potential customer or client sounds keen, go for it! Arrange to meet him or her to show your product or explain more about your service.

### 4. MEET UP

Arrange a time and place to meet that's convenient for your potential customer or client. Be professional, but also likeable. They're equally important characteristics when making a sale.

If the customer agrees the deal, bring the meeting to a fairly speedy end. Your job is done – for now. It's time to head home and deliver on the promise you made with your first customer.

### 5. MAKE SOME NOISE

Once you've made your first sale – shout about it! If your new customer or client agrees, include them in a press release or write about them on your website or blog, so other potential customers or clients can see that you're well and truly in business! (More on this in the marketing chapters later.)

# Taking payment

An important point to be considered is how you will take payment. Most people will want to pay by cash or credit/debit card. Think about how you will offer this.

### CASH

Accepting cash is fairly straightforward. All you'll need to do is set up a small float to provide change and some way of recording sales. The float doesn't have to be enormous – look at the prices you are selling your products for and plan accordingly (round numbers are easiest to deal with). It is a good idea to take along a receipt book so that you can write out receipts for anyone paying cash.

An inventory list will also be invaluable here as this will enable you to keep track of what stock is selling – useful for evaluating sales after the fair and also to keep you on top of what stock is remaining.

## CREDIT AND DEBIT CARD PAYMENTS

An exciting development in the payment space is the ability for small businesses to accept card payments via their smartphones. At this stage, there are two main providers in the UK, with Foursquare and PayPal set to enter the market soon.

The way these mobile payments work is very simple.

Through Intuit Pay (**www.intuit.co.uk/mobile-payment-solutions**) you can take debit and credit card payments anywhere. Only two steps are required to get started. Step one is to register, followed by step two which involves downloading the free app and following instructions.

Intuit Pay is currently in pilot mode and only works on Android phones. With it, you can accept in-person payments with the app and associated chip-and-PIN card reader. You can also log in and process card payments instantly online. Funds are guaranteed immediately and deposited to your bank account within a few days. There is no set-up fee to join Intuit Pay and there is a choice of two payment plans:

- pay as you go with a 3% charge on each transaction
- pay a subscription of £10/month and a fee of just 2% per transaction (the best option if you think that you will be making total transactions of over £1,000/month).

Most applications are instantly approved, meaning you can use Intuit Pay on your mobile as soon as you receive the card reader or immediately through the online terminal. However, for some people the application may be pended whilst checks are carried out. This may take a couple of days.

In the case of iZettle (**www.izettle.com**), you launch the app on your device (either smartphone or tablet) enter the cost of the item, a short description of the item you're selling and perhaps even take a picture of it. If you are using the app on a tablet device, you can also choose the item you are selling directly from a product gallery where you have already organised the items by adding names, photos and prices. You then just insert the buyer's debit or credit card in the card reader and tap 'Pay'. Your customer signs on your device screen to confirm their purchase and that's it! The system can also send a receipt to his or her email address when the purchase is complete.

The service is available for both businesses and individuals, and consists of a free iOS and Android app and a mini chip-card reader, which costs just £20 (you get £20 of free transactions in return).

• Set-up fee: One-time payment of £20 for mini chip-card reader.

• Transaction fees: For the UK, 2.75% on each transaction.

# BEAUTIFUL BUSINESS: HOME RESTYLER

**Name:** Katey Korzenietz

**Business:** Home Restyler

**Website:** www.homerestyler.co.uk

**Social media:** @home_restyler | www.facebook.com/home.restyler | www.pinterest.com/homerestyler

Katey Korzenietz's business Home Restyler was created in April 2010, born out of her life-long passion for home interiors and her fascination with changing and re-styling room layouts and colour schemes.

> "I can happily spend hours rearranging furniture and objects around people's houses, playing with ideas to create new looks. I never get tired of it. I have a natural instinct for styling and am always on the lookout for new ways to create impactful spaces."

One of the first things Katey did when she set up her business was to send out an email to everyone she knew, explaining what she was doing, who the business was aimed at and the services she was offering.

> "Within 24 hours I had my first email requesting further information, which then led on to one of my biggest projects to-date."

Since then, Katey has looked for other ways to promote the business. Reputation and word of mouth are key.

> "Word of mouth is the winner in this game. I have also been fortunate to be asked to write for *Devon Life* magazine and other local publications (off the back of my blog), which helps build my reputation and trust in the Home Restyler brand. I sometimes attend networking events. And I always have a business card to hand as you never know who you might meet, especially when out socialising!"

As well as running the business, Katey also has a young daughter. She runs her business in a way that suits both of them.

"Until my daughter attends school full time I am happy to keep my client base limited to a maximum of two at any one time. That way, I am focused on delivering on-brief without stretching myself too far. Once I am able to work full time I will focus more on advertising and marketing activities to extend my customer base and will spend time photographing past projects to expand the image library on my online portfolio. In this line of work, customers are keen to see lots of previous work, whether for reassurance or just out of interest to see what I am able to do."

Although she mostly works alone, Katey has built up a network of reliable contacts and now always works with the same curtain and blind designer/maker. She also uses social media to get ideas and inspiration from others in the same area of work.

"If I need inspiration I get online and put ideas out there. I always get great feedback and hints from others within the industry."

Katey has big plans for Home Restyler in 2013:

"I want to continue to strengthen my position, better communicate Home Restyler's point of difference and keep spreading the Home Restyler word. Come September 2013 I'll be full time so it will be full steam ahead!"

# Top tips!

1. "Think big – get all your ideas on paper, be wild and imaginative and once you've got it all off your chest, rein it in and be realistic."

2. "Make sure you understand the market you want to enter, research your competitors – why are they or aren't they doing well?"

3. "Be prepared – do everything you need for a successful launch *before* you launch. First impressions count and you want people to remember who you are, what you do and why you stand out from your competitors for all the right reasons."

4. "Lastly, if you don't try it you'll never know. Just make sure it's a viable business and not just something you personally are passionate about. To make money you need others to love it too!"

# SELLING INTO PHYSICAL STORES

Maybe you've started by selling products direct to customers, but what about making sales via local shops?

Before you approach any shops, make a list of appropriate places where you think your product could work well. For example, does your town have a gift shop or art gallery, are there lots of boutiques that stock a range of different items?

It's a good idea to also think outside the box. For example, could your local coffee shop stock some of your items, or perhaps use branded samples on the tables?

## Pop-ups

Want to hone retail skills, meet customers face to face and make sales? Why not try a high street pop-up and test new markets in the flesh?

PopUp Britain (**www.popupbritain.co.uk**) was created to give new British brands an opportunity to get onto the high street and fill empty shops with small business activity. Their flagship pop-up store in Richmond opened in July 2012 and has since welcomed start-ups and small businesses who trade in the shop for a fortnight before moving on to allow new businesses to move in.

The PopUp tenants are all online businesses that don't normally have the budget to take on a shop single-handedly and full time. PopUp Britain brings tenants together to share the cost and workload. Following success in Richmond, the scheme is expanding across the UK.

The project has delivered a national 'PopUp Lease' (thanks to Nick Darby at SNR Denton) which makes contractual arrangements with landlords a whole lot simpler. And with support from Minister for Housing and High Streets, Mark Prisk, a PopUp should be coming to a town near you soon.

## THE ART OF THE POP

Here's how to ensure your pop-up experience is a profitable one.

- **Place** – choose a premises in a location that suits your products and is populated with people who represent your target market.

- **Offer** – ahead of moving in, prepare sufficient stock at a price that's right for the particular area. Present the products in a way that will attract customers' attention. Consider your own presentation and body language when approaching and dealing with customers.

- **Promote** – now you're in the shop, tell people you're there! Promote your presence to existing customers through social media. To attract new trade, consider partnerships with neighbouring retailers, flyers in the train station, releases to the local press and pop-up parties, lock-ins, cook-offs and pottery shows, to deliver a retail experience that customers will never forget!

# 5 top tips for market placement

*Laura Rigney, founder of PitcherHouse and Mumpreneur UK, is author of* Pitching Products for Small Business. *Here are her five top tips for pitching your products effectively . . .*

## 1. BE CONFIDENT WITH PRICING

"Selling in wholesale is a whole new ballpark as far as pricing is concerned. Make your product attractive to buyers with your pricing. A great way to show you're trying to help retailers is to set up a structured pricing system, i.e. 100 units or less £xx per unit, 101–500 units £xx per unit and 501 units or more £xx per unit. This system could also encourage shops and buyers to place larger orders."

## 2. UNDERSTAND YOUR PRODUCT INSIDE OUT

"Understanding your product thoroughly means being on top of technical data as well as knowing why someone would buy it. When you get a meeting with a buyer or approach a shop owner, talk with confidence about where the product is made, by who, and using what kind of materials. Remember there is pressure on large retailers to 'go green', so the more you can offer that as a potential supplier the more attractive you will be."

## 3. BE PREPARED

"If a buyer places an order, how quickly will you have manufacturing, distribution and storage in place? Buyers won't expect a new small business to have a giant factory sitting waiting for someone to press the 'go' button but they will want a realistic estimate of how long it will be until your product is in their warehouses/on the shop shelf. Once you have given your timings, stick to them. Even if this means exaggerating the time it will take for them to be delivered. Better to be early rather than late!"

## 4. PITCH PERFECT

"If you're pitching in person, make it informative, exciting and interesting and where possible have evidence of past sales and customer satisfaction. You need to know your figures without having to look through paperwork and be prepared to haggle a little on prices. If someone likes your product enough and you have sold it well enough they will buy it even if it's a few pennies more than they would like to pay. In the other direction, sometimes it may be worth offering a larger than normal discount as a trial for their first order."

## 5. STAY LISTED

"When a company takes on your product it's called being listed. Once you are listed the work is just beginning! It is now time to stay listed for as long as possible and the way to do this is through marketing and PR. The more you promote your product and the shops/galleries/boutiques that are selling them, the more they will be bought by consumers, thus encouraging buyers to place more orders with you!"

# 9 sales tips for the craft and creative industry

*Jackie Wade, MD of Winning Sales and author of* Successful Selling for Small Business, *gives her top 12 tips for face-to-face sales success . . .*

## 1. THINK OF SELLING IN THE POSITIVE AND GOOD OLD-FASHIONED CONTEXT OF 'SALES ASSISTANT'

"You don't have to be pushy, aggressive or in-your-face to be successful at selling. You need to focus instead on helping or assisting your customers to buy well and hopefully that means buy you."

## 2. SEEK TO ENGAGE WITH YOUR POTENTIAL CUSTOMERS

"Smile, be warm and friendly and above all be natural. Be you. Don't be aloof or put physical barriers in the way. If you're selling on a stall or at an exhibition or standing behind a table or counter, come around and stand next to your customer. Seek to connect through your body language and eye contact."

## 3. TALK TO YOUR CUSTOMERS – DON'T SELL AT THEM

"Ask them simple things like 'How are you enjoying the day?', 'Have you made any interesting purchases so far?' Build rapport, than seek to chat about their specific needs in relation to your product – who's it for, what's the occasion, when is it . . . 'How can I help you today?' Be careful about talking too much or trying to tell them too much about your product. Tell them what they need to know and focus on the key benefits."

## 4. LISTEN TO YOUR POTENTIAL CUSTOMERS

"Ask them about their needs and wants before offering the product you think is right. Don't try and sell until you understand them and their situation and then seek to match the right product to the right customer."

## 5. SEEK FEEDBACK

"Don't be afraid to ask 'What do you think?', 'Is this the kind of thing you're looking for?' You need to be getting positive feedback if you are going to close successfully and get the sale. If you are receiving positive feedback or noticing positive body language or buying signals (nods, gestures, smile), don't forget to ask for the business. 'So would you be happy to buy one and try it out?', 'Would you like me to book in an appointment to come and look at your house and we can discuss colours . . ?' Sometimes people need a little gentle nudge to take action. This is not the same as being pushy – it's encouragement."

## 6. DON'T FEEL UNDER PRESSURE TO DROP YOUR PRICE OR BARTER

"If people say something seems a little dear, ask (not through gritted teeth!) 'I'd be interested to know why you feel that/think that?' Explain the value of what you do and be confident about your price. Offer extras if you must but avoid discounting as it devalues you and your product. Remember, it's not a car boot sale!"

## 7. DON'T FORGET ADDED VALUE SALES

"Can you cross-sell and sell two or three items instead of one? Try not to be shy, people are often happy to know that one thing goes nicely with something else. 'We have lovely cushions to match those rugs'. Don't forget, people can always say no. Even then, it's not personal. Generally, people like to receive good and genuine advice and tips. Be proactive, don't wait to be asked."

## 8. REMEMBER YOU ARE AN IMPORTANT PART OF YOUR PRODUCT

"Make sure you share your expertise, uniqueness and history, if it helps to add value to the product or purchase. Again don't be afraid to blow your own trumpet in the nicest possible way. No one else will. And remember – look the part!"

## 9. ALWAYS BE THINKING ABOUT FUTURE SALES

"If someone buys today, let them know where and how they can buy again. Ask them to recommend or introduce other people they know to you and your product. They will happily do that if they like you. If they don't buy today, how can they reconnect with you when they are ready or when they change their mind? Make it easy for people to find and buy from you. It will greatly increase the return you get from your investment to participate at an event."

# SELLING ON PLATFORM SITES

Raise profile and make sales via powerful platform sites before creating your own (see Chapter Nine). Whether selling boutique crafts or interior design solutions, there are a number of options. The upside is these sites attract customers on your behalf, and some of them attract customers from all over the world. (The downside is that they charge a commission, and sometimes a listing fee, on products sold.)

## EBAY

eBay (**www.eBay.co.uk**) has grown to become the largest shopping mall on the web. There are around 180,000 registered businesses trading on the site in the UK, generating billions of pounds worth of sales. Having a store on eBay means you are opened up to an international audience and lots of potential customers.

*eBay expert, Dan Wilson (***www.wilsondan.co.uk***), offers five tips on how to make the most of the mega marketplace known as eBay . . .*

TIPS { eBay advice

**1. Start small**

"Go slow until you've found your way. Start with a few, easy-to-post items and learn about eBay before boosting your range and prices. Don't stake too much on your first eBay bet."

**2. Sell like you mean it**

"The eBay marketplace is competitive and you'll lose out unless you have top-notch listings. Craft fabulous item titles, make impeccable pictures and write descriptions that tempt buyers. Be truthful and honest and look professional from the start."

### 3. Be quick off the mark

"Buyers have come to expect great service. Dispatch orders quickly – preferably within 24 hours of payment – and well-packed, and make sure you reply to emails and other communications swiftly, too. The quality and speed of your replies and dispatches has an impact on customer feedback."

### 4. Put a lid on postal costs

"Understand postage and packaging costs and make sure you factor it in to your costs where necessary."

### 5. Loyalty means profit

"When you're building your eBay business, encouraging repeat buyers is important. Once a buyer trusts you as an online seller, they're likely to keep coming back. Offer discounts and incentives with every dispatch and cross-market complementary products."

## ENTERPRISE NATION

The Enterprise Nation Directory connects your business services with business buyers. We refer to it as the friendliest business-to-business marketplace on the web.

You can list your business in the directory for just £20 for the year. It's supported by a business blog, with tips and advice on sales and marketing, IT efficiency, productivity and motivation, and a community for all the help and support you need to start and grow your business.

## ALIBABA

Having a presence on Alibaba (**www.alibaba.com**) enables you to buy and sell and source supplies with companies from across the globe. The site has visitors from 240 countries and regions, with over 660,000 registered users in the UK. Through the site you can locate suppliers or make sales of your finished product direct to customers.

## ISTOCKPHOTO

Want to sell your photography, illustrations, videos or music effects around the world? iStockphoto (**www.istockphoto.com**) is the site for you:

> "iStockphoto is the web's original source for royalty-free stock images, media and design elements. For over 10 years artists, designers and photographers from all over the world have come here to create, work and learn."

To start selling, all you have to do is join the site, apply to be a contributor and submit samples of your work. As a contributor, you receive a base royalty rate of 20% for each file downloaded, which goes up to 40% if you exclusively display work on the site.

# Handmade marketplaces

A growing number of sites are dedicated to helping the artisan and handmade business owner sell goods across the globe.

## ETSY

> "The world's handmade marketplace"

*How does it work?*

1. You list the item on Etsy (**www.etsy.com**) for a fee. It costs 20 cents (roughly 12p) to list an item for four months.

2. Shoppers then find your item and purchase it from you directly, using your payment system which you have set up with Etsy, for example PayPal. Etsy takes a 3.5% transaction fee from the total sale price of each sale.

3. You then ship the item directly to your customer.

*Getting started*

Setting up a shop on Etsy is easy and should only take a few minutes: **www.etsy.com/join**

You will need to enter your Etsy username here, which will be displayed to customers looking at your products. Remember to think about your branding and how you want to present yourself to potential customers when entering these details.

*Paying fees*

All of your fees will be paid using the credit card you list when you register, or the PayPal account you link to your Etsy account. Etsy will calculate your fees on a monthly basis and email you with a list of payments that are due. You can also pay your bill manually through your account.

*Community*

Etsy has a thriving community where sellers, artists and creators all come together to share their work and ideas with one another. Etsy also runs events like Craft Nights, which could be a great way to meet others and promote your products to a receptive audience.

The site has a blog which highlights new product launches and initiatives, plus featured sellers and debates on various topics.

Forums feature strongly on the site, so if you need advice, look here – there will always be someone who can help you find what you need!

Etsy have recently launched a free eBook called 'Getting Started on Etsy' to guide you through the process of becoming a seller. You can download a copy at: **www.etsy.me/ GettingStartedOnEtsy**

## NOT ON THE HIGH STREET

"One basket, hundreds of unique shops"

*How does it work?*

Not On The High Street (**www.notonthehighstreet.com**) offers you the chance to promote and sell your products under the umbrella of their brand and be supported by their in-house team. They look after all of the e-commerce, administration and marketing elements of selling through the site, so all you need to worry about are the products.

Not On The High Street differs from a number of other platform sites in that they are very selective about who sells with them and *decline over 90% of applications*. Membership packages vary but the basic package allows you to add 30 products to your own store, with your own logo, company name and URL.

*Getting started*

If you're interested in getting set up with NOTHS, the first thing you will need to do is to take some photographs of your products and submit these using the online application form.

Applications can take up to seven working days to be processed. After that time you will be contacted by a member of the team.

## FOLKSY

"Folksy is a place to buy handmade things, and for makers to sell their work and find supplies. Based in the UK, Folksy aims to reclaim craft and showcase talented makers and their work."

Interestingly, you can sell craft supplies on Folksy (**www.folksy.com**) as well as handmade goods, so long as they are listed as 'supplies' and not in the 'handmade' category and this also applies to Etsy.

*How does it work?*

1. You list the item on Folksy for a fee. It costs 20p to list an item for 180 days or until the item is sold.

2. Shoppers find your item and purchase it from you directly, using your payment system which you have set up with Folksy, for example PayPal, or you can accept other payments, such as cash or cheque at your own discretion. Folksy takes a 5% commission fee from the total value of each sale.

3. You then ship the item directly to your customer.

*Getting started*

The first thing you need to do is to decide on the username for your shop. This can't be changed so think carefully about your branding and how you want to appear to prospective customers.

Once your item is listed, customers can start viewing and purchasing. When an order is received you will get an order from Folksy with all the buyer's details and the information about the product ordered. You will also receive an email from PayPal to say payment has been completed. You then ship the product directly to the customer.

*Paying fees*

You settle fees through the Your Account section of the website. The total shown will be made up of billed and unbilled fees as well as the 5% commission on sales.

*Community*

Folksy features a blog which gives updates on important news and events. The site also has a forum where members can discuss craft tips, as well as events, ideas for your shopfront and anything else that takes your fancy!

## ICRAFT

"Creativity without borders"

*How does it work?*

First you need to set up an account with iCraft (**www.icraft.ca**) which costs CAD$25 (there's about 60p to the Canadian dollar at the time of writing). This is a one-off fee to register and ensure your identity.

You then decide on which membership package you would like from the following:

- 1 to 5 products – free but advertising will appear at the bottom of your page
- **Starter** – 5 to 50 items. CAD$5/month. Every additional item is CAD$0.20/month.
- **Professional** – 5 to 100 items. CAD$10.00 /month. Every additional item is CAD$0.20/month.
- **Elite** – Unlimited items. CAD$15.00 /month.

Shoppers find your item and place an order. iCraft will process all payments through PayPal and notify you of the payment deposit. You don't pay any commission to iCraft for this, or for the sale of the product. You ship the item directly to your customer.

*Getting started*

You can set up your shop with iCraft at: **www.icraft.ca/registration.php**

*Community*

iCraft features the Handmade Community where members get together to share their love of all things handmade. The community features message boards to discuss ideas, share tips and generally support each other, while Blog Central publishes helpful articles and topical news.

## DAWANDA

"DaWanda is the place for unique and individual products and people. Buy handmade and hard to find goods, share your discoveries with your friends and create your own collections."

*How does it work?*

List your items on DaWanda (**en.dawanda.com**) and set up your own shop which gives you the option of a direct URL – nice and easy to promote to your customers!

People will browse your listings and when someone orders a product you receive an email. You check the details of the order, making a note of any special requests from the buyer, and once happy to go ahead you click to confirm the order, so the buyer can see the final price and pay you. You then ship the item directly to the customer using the method you have specified in the listing.

*Getting started*

With DaWanda you can set up your own shop for free – all you need to do is provide a name and set up 20 shop categories. You can create your own shop window at this stage to show off the key items in your shop. As soon as this has been set up, you can start listing your items and selling to customers!

DaWanda also features something called the DaWanda widget, a tool for displaying your shop on your own website or blog.

*Paying fees*

DaWanda charges a 5% commission on all sales but does not charge for listing products. Once your fees reach a minimum of €5, DaWanda will email you an invoice with instructions on how to pay.

*Community*

The website features the News Bulletin Board as well as a blog, ideal for getting all the latest information on what DaWanda offers and what's popular on the site. The forums are a great place to chat with other crafters and there are also video, social media and Gift Detective areas.

## ARTFIRE

"The Premier handmade marketplace to buy and sell handmade crafts, supplies, vintage and art."

*How does it work?*

Set up your shop on Artfire (**www.artfire.com**) and list as many items as you want, with up to ten photographs per item.

The customer will browse your shop and place an order. You receive the customer's payment and also their delivery details in order to ship the product.

*Getting started*

You can set up your shop for free at: **www.artfire.com/ext/register/account**

You then pay nothing for 30 days, and after that the rate is £7.56 a month for unlimited listings. ArtFire do not take a commission on sales.

*Paying fees*

Fees will be taken from your nominated payment card on the same day each month (the one on which you originally signed up). For example, if you joined on the 5th December, you would be charged your monthly fee on the 5th of every month.

*Community*

ArtfFre has a range of different community options for you to get involved in and interact with other members. There are forums where you can communicate and share ideas with other crafters, as well as ArtDaily, which is an opportunity to learn new crafts and get sound business advice, plus there's the chance to join a guild and earn a guild badge, as well as listen to the weekly podcast from John Jacobs and Tony Ford, giving tips on how to promote your business and use Artfire to its full potential.

## MISI (MAKE IT, SELL IT)

"The home of buying and selling handmade in the UK."

*How does it work?*

Create a shop with Misi (**www.misi.co.uk**) and list your items for free. Customers can then browse through your shop and purchase items. When you sell a product you will receive an email notification from Misi which will prompt you to log in to see the full details of the sale. Payment can either be by cheque or PayPal, and once payment is received, you ship the product direct to the customer.

*Paying fees*

Misi charges 20p per listing, which will be added to your account as soon as you start listing items. Misi also take a 3% commission fee on every sale and this is also added to your account. Fees are then payable on a monthly basis.

*Community*

The Misi community section is broken down into several areas including: a blog where crafters write about their latest ideas, materials and events; a forum for sharing tips and ideas; and a Meet the Maker section where shop-owners and crafters are encouraged to share their experiences with the community.

## SHOPHANDMADE

"Rewarding Creativity."

*How does it work?*

You can sell your items on ShopHandmade (**www.shophandmade.com**) in five easy steps! Once you have listed your products, customers can browse them and begin buying right away.

When an item sells you will be notified by email, and payment will be made to your registered PayPal account. You then ship the item using the easy-to-print labels through PayPal.

*Getting started*

Firstly, you need to list your item for a small fee of 25 cents, and then upload up to five photos per item. Then you need to decide if you are participating in Sales and Galleries and activate your listing.

When you are listing items, there is also the opportunity to get the listing sponsored, which means a third-party sponsor will pay for listing your item, costing you nothing. There are several sponsors to choose from and their sponsorship simply means that a non-intrusive advertisement will appear on your product page.

*Paying fees*

ShopHandmade only charge a percentage of the item's final selling price if you have chosen to do this. The payment is taken when the item actually sells.

*Community*

ShopHandmade features blogs from various sellers so that you can see what other crafters are up to and keep track of developments and new ideas in the crafting world.

TIP { A platform presence

Even if you are selling via another platform site, you still need to promote your online presence in these places. So make sure to add your Etsy/eBay/Folksy etc. URL to business cards, email signatures and social media pages.

# POSTAGE AND PACKAGING

Postage and packaging is a big issue for small creative businesses so you'll want to work out the best way to structure this, as Caroline from Patchwork Harmony knows:

> "I ran into difficulty with this when I first started Patchwork Harmony, as I was offering a fixed rate – I had a rate for UK, one for Europe and one for international – but I would get a really large, heavy order from someone in the States who may only have paid £9.95 for postage when in reality it cost me £40 to post!"

A key thing to decide is how you will structure the charges for postage and packaging on your website. For example, will there be a fixed rate price to certain territories, or will this be dependent on the weight or size of the order? Work out how much it's going to cost you to send items to customers to ensure you're not eating into profits.

It's also important to note that some of the platform sites might only offer a standard postage rate and in reality this might not cover the postage costs of heavier items. Consider working this into the price of the item itself, without the product becoming too expensive and putting off the customer.

Free postage on your own website is an option and a way to do this might be to add these costs on to the total price of the item. If customers think they are getting postage for free it may encourage them to click 'buy' even if the price of the item is slightly higher.

## Which delivery service to use?

Consider which type of postal/courier service you want to use. Think about whether you'll have time to go to the Post Office each day to post orders (and if not, be clear on your site what delivery times will be) or will it be easier to organise a collection service?

For business customers, Royal Mail offers a collection service and favourable postage rates. If sending high-value items, it might be better to send these via courier which can often offer insurance and guaranteed delivery times. Use the parcel price comparison sites referenced below to get the best deal.

- Royal Mail Business | www.royalmail.com/delivery
- Parcel Monkey | www.parcelmonkey.co.uk
- Parcel Checker | www.parcelchecker.co.uk
- Parcel2Go | www.parcel2go.com
- DHL | www.dhl.co.uk
- FedEx | www.fedex.com
- TNT | www.tnt.com
- UPS | www.ups.com

# The world of brown paper and string

Packaging is also an important part of selling online. If selling breakable items, ensure you have suitable packaging. You'll almost certainly need different sized boxes and plenty of bubble-wrap to accommodate varying order sizes and fragility. Source these items *in bulk* online to save a lot of money.

Alongside secure packaging, consider your presentation. Imagine how thrilled your customers will be to receive a well-presented and carefully wrapped item inside their delivery! This doesn't need to be costly – some pretty coloured tissue paper tied with string is effective, or get creative and wrap items in anything from old magazine pages found at a car boot sale, to plain parcel paper printed with a rubber stamp personalized with your company logo.

Be sure to pop in a business card or a promotional/discount flyer to entice customers back to your store. Include your website details, blog URL and Twitter handle so customers can look you up after receiving the order – and spread the word to others. They may not have 'followed' you when they placed the order so this gives another chance to increase your social media following too.

# YOUR PRODUCTS IN FOCUS

Increase the chances of having your products browsed and bought by uploading quality photos of your items.

Successful eBay sellers Mark and Philomena have seen first-hand the power of having professional images and how this translates into sales. With this experience, they have set up a new company – Business Photography – to help you take your best shot . . .

 There are basically two options for producing images of product: do it yourself or bring in a professional.

### DIY – THE SELLER OF SINGLE SMALL ITEMS

If you are selling single items below a value of £100, you should be taking your own pictures. Why? Simply because your profit margin will not soak up the cost of a professional commercial photographer whose prices are typically going to range from £15 to £20 for a single image (lower for multiples).

Whilst you will not be able to equal the image quality that a professional provides, you will be able to supply acceptable quality images if you invest in a good basic setup.

Our recommendation for equipment:

• A bridge camera with macro and minimum 10mp (Fuji make some good bridge cameras, £200–£300) and a good tripod (£80).

• A light tent (purchase the largest you can fit on a table – 100cm cubed is a good size for small to medium sized product, £25–£40 should get a decent quality tent).

• Continuous lights with stands (daylight balanced) – with as much power as you can afford (more light = faster shutter speeds), expect to pay £200 for about 2400w of light.

• An image editor like Lightroom 3 which will enable you to batch process images quickly – £220 (you could use Gimp which is free but it will not be as quick with batch processing, we imagine).

Adobe Photoshop is the industry standard for image editing and Photoshop Elements is a simpler version.

- A decent computer that can handle lots of images being edited at once – minimum spec: Windows 7, 4GB of RAM, decent processor and an external drive for storage of the images.

- Preferably – an area dedicated to photography, so that your set-up is ready for use continuously.

## SET-UP

- Choose a mid-tone grey background for the backdrop in your tent. White backgrounds (pure white) are very hard to achieve and take professional-level skills, whereas a mid-tone is forgiving and will give a background to contrast with a light or dark item, enabling high turnover of images produced.

- Do not use bright colours as your background. They produce strong colour casts; white should look white, a red background will make white look pink.

- Remove/blank all sources of light other than the daylight bulb lighting. This stops lots of lighting problems.

- Set your lights so that you have one shining on top of the tent and two to one side to create some contrast in the tent.

- Set your camera to its auto mode with macro and shoot in JPEG.

- When taking the images, think about your framing of the image. Get it right in the camera so that you don't need to crop it afterwards using software.

- Keep your set-up consistent and your images will remain consistent.

- Bulk edit in Lightroom and make sure that when you export your images you reduce them to a standard web resolution size (640 × 640 is a good middle ground we feel).

## BRING IN THE PROFESSIONAL – THE SELLER OF MULTIPLE QUANTITY ITEMS

Have you ever heard the saying that 'accountants pay for themselves'? A professional commercial photographer can do the very same thing; they produce images that help you sell your product because they know how to portray quality and professionalism. They invest substantial sums to deliver this level of quality through equipment and knowledge.

The cost of producing the images needs to be proportionally small to the sales attached to that image; one image for £20 that helps sell 300 items is not expensive.

Quality of image helps differentiate between competitors – look at the competition, how good are their images? Now compare yours. Examine the market leaders and the trendy e-commerce giants who tend to invest in high quality images.

The type of seller that should use professional help will probably be selling cross platform on many sites and be handling large ranges of stock and will be looking for growth.

The images produced should meet certain criteria:

- Pure white background – the industry standard in the majority of cases.

- High contrast and colour-corrected images (eBay are considering using contrast in images as a factor in Best Match; third party platform companies like you to have good images).

- Branding in the form of subtle watermarking can again be used to support marketing, as can your consistent style.

## FINDING A PROFESSIONAL COMMERCIAL PHOTOGRAPHER

- Ascertain their skill-set in this niche area of commercial photography – they should have a website with examples of their product shots which you can examine.

- Understand what they provide for the price, and make sure basic colour correction, white balancing and removal of flaws is included – you do not want to be handed half-finished images that need more money spent on them to make them usable.

- Find a specialist in commercial photography – a wedding photographer will not be equipped to supply commercial product photography as a rule, neither will the 'friend with a camera'.

- Make sure that the photographer has the equipment to shoot on your premises if you have large runs as this will reduce transport costs.

- Negotiate price discounts if you are requesting hundreds of images.

We hope you find this a good introductory guide. If you need extra help or advice on this subject please feel free to contact Mark or Philomena at Business Photography (**www.business-photography.biz**).

*Content adapted and with permission from a post originally appearing on Tamebay:*
**tamebay.com/2011/10/e-commerce-and-photography**

Another option is to use a photography student or a photographer who is keen to build their portfolio, as long as you are happy for them to also display the images on their own website.

It's a really good idea to shoot pack shots of your products as well as lifestyle images of them in use. This not only makes the products more enticing and appealing to the customer as they can see it 'in situ', but it is also a great publicity tool as magazine editors and bloggers love beautifully styled images that they can put straight on their pages. It is worth investing in this or getting the help from a budding amateur stylist if you can. As well as checking out local universities or colleges for student photographers, it can also be worth networking via social media to find suitable people to help you.

## Distance Selling Regulations

One thing to bear in mind when selling goods or services to consumers via the internet, mail order or by phone, is compliance with the Consumer Protection (Distance Selling) Regulations 2000. The key features of the regulations are:

- You must offer consumers clear information including details of the goods or services offered, delivery arrangements and payment, the supplier's details and the consumer's cancellation right before they buy (known as prior information). This information should be provided in writing.

- The consumer has a period of seven working days from delivery of the items to cancel their contract with you.

- These regulations only apply when selling to consumers, as opposed to businesses. In the event of a contract being ceased, you have to refund money, including delivery charges, within 30 days of the date of cancellation.

For more guidance, see: **tinyurl.com/63798kq**

Keep customers coming back with offers and good service and attract new customers by making some noise and rising up the search engine ranks!

# Chapter Nine
## YOUR ONLINE
# HOME

YOU'VE STARTED MAKING sales via platform sites and feel it's time to create your own home on the web. Your site is a powerful marketing tool and a way to make money. Having the right technology and knowledge allows you to build, develop and maintain your site. And you can do it all in-house.

# BUILDING YOUR DOTCOM HQ

You can create a home on the web through having your own website that you have built to your own requirements or by investing in a template website. Let's look at both options.

## DIY

You have decided to build your own site or have a developer take care of it for you. The first thing to do is buy a domain, i.e. a URL.

There are lots of domain registration companies whose websites allow you to check for available domain names and often suggest available alternatives. Here are three options.

- 1&1 | **www.1and1.co.uk**
- 123-reg | **www.123-reg.co.uk**
- Easily.co.uk | **www.easily.co.uk**

Remember it is important that you choose your business name and domain name at the same time. You don't want to choose a great business name and then discover that the domain is taken. It is also worth checking if the Twitter handle you want is available at this point, as you want to keep coherency across your online platforms.

Registering a domain name doesn't give you a website, just an address for it (and an email address). Think of it like reserving a car parking space. You've got the space, now you need to buy the car!

A hosting company will sort you out with the web space to host your website. This is measured in megabytes and gigabytes, just like the information on your computer. You upload the files that make up a website – pictures and pages – to this space, so that the rest of the world can see them.

In terms of how much web space you will need, basic hosting packages offer about 250MB of web space, but anything over 1 or 2GB is more sensible and it will also allow you to handle more traffic on your website as it grows more popular.

With a domain name and web space, potential customers should be able to type your website address into their browser and find out all about your business – just as soon as you've built your site. Finding a hosting company shouldn't be hard. Most domain registration companies, including those mentioned above, offer web space as a package and vice versa.

When it comes to hiring a designer, have a think about what you'd like your website to do for your business. The easiest way to start is to think of your website as a brochure, but remember to include the following pages at the very least.

- About us

- News

- Products or services

- FAQs (Frequently Asked Questions)

- Contact us

Choose a designer who has carried out work you like the look of and for companies in a similar kind of sector to your own. That way, the designer will understand what site you're after – and what your kind of visitor will be looking for, as well as how they like to browse and buy. Check out the Enterprise Nation Directory (**www.enterprisenation.com**) or similar sites to find the right web designer for you.

## HOW TO BRIEF A WEB DESIGNER/DEVELOPER

*Here is Emily Hewett's (***www.birdsontheblog.co.uk***) advice on how best to brief a web designer/developer . . .*

" When working with a designer you need to have a coherent brief for them to follow. Here are my hints and tips to help you be clear in your mind what it is you want so you can communicate this to your designer and use the brief as a point of reference throughout the project.

- **Who are you?** – even if the designer has worked with your organisation previously, always give them a short summary of your company; who you are and what you do. This will help refresh their memory and tune in to your particular industry sector. You will also need to tell them about your market and how you fit in to the larger scheme of things, for example who your competitors are both locally and nationally.

- **What do you want to achieve?** – you need to detail the purpose, for example are you wanting to capture data, generate sales, increase footfall, etc.

- **Who are you talking to?** – outline a profile of who your customer is. The designer will need to know whether they are targeting females, males or both, what is the age group of the audience, what is their average income and what's their location.

- **What tone are you using?** – deciding on how you speak to your audience is important. You may be writing the copy yourself or you may have a copywriter to do this for you. In this section of the brief tell the designer if it's a laidback chatty tone or a formal, informative tone. The tone of the copy will affect the design and these two elements need to gel to produce a successful end product.

- **What are your likes and dislikes?** – provide examples to the designer wherever possible of what you like or don't like online. It might be a certain colour palette or illustration style or it could be a format. Any of these things help the designer get into your head and understand what it is that you require, making for a better working relationship.

- **Are there any mandatory elements?** – tell the designer if there are any mandatory fonts, colours, logos, legal text, images, etc. so that they can make sure they are producing something on brand that adheres to your corporate image.

- **What's your budget?** – this doesn't need to be set in stone and a good designer won't take a large budget and fit a job to it, they should find the most cost-effective way of producing exactly what you want, but if you have a small budget the designer will have to make decisions based on what they can realistically achieve in that price bracket.

- **When do you want it?** – make the designer aware of your ultimate deadline that needs to be achieved.

- **Have you covered everything?** – show the brief to a colleague or friend to see if they understand the content and once happy with the brief, send or talk it through with your designer and invite questions so they are aware you are approachable and that you are both working from the same list of requirements.

Doing this not only creates a good bond between you and your designer, it also helps you clarify what you really want from your website.

# Template site

If DIY sounds too much like hard work, there are a good number of companies offering template websites that come with domain registration, hosting, e-commerce and a basic level of design as part of the package.

There are a number of template site providers offering websites that can be set up today and trading by tomorrow. Check out these options:

- Moonfruit | **www.moonfruit.com**
- Create | **www.create.net**
- Magento | **www.magentocommerce.com**
- Shopify | **www.shopify.com**

# 5 tips for making your website legally compliant

*These tips are offered by Joanna Tall, founder of* **OffToSeeMyLawyer.com** *. . .*

## 1. DISPLAY TERMS OF USE

"Think of your website like a board game you are about to play with your visitors. They arrive and are ready to play and you need to state the rules or else it will be chaos! So, for example, state what they can and cannot do, e.g. may they copy your materials? May they rely on the information you provide without double-checking with you or elsewhere? What liability are you prepared to accept? Provide a link to your terms of use, ideally on every page of your website or under a 'Legals' section."

## 2. DISPLAY YOUR PRIVACY POLICY

"Most websites collect personal data about their visitors either by getting them to register on the site or sign up for a newsletter. By law you must tell visitors what you will be doing with this data and the best way to do this is to set out the information in a so-called privacy policy. Again, a link to it on every page is best. More complex rules apply if you plan to collect sensitive information or information from children, or want to pass the information to third parties; for this you should consult a lawyer. Additionally, you are likely to need to register as a data processor under the Data Protection Act. Simply go to **www.ico.gov.uk** for more information."

## 3. IF SELLING GOODS OR SERVICES ONLINE, DISPLAY YOUR TERMS OF SALE

"Just as with the board game example, you need rules for selling your goods or services. Most importantly, you need to get your visitors to acknowledge that they accept them. So ideally get them to tick a box stating that they accept them before they proceed to check out. You also need to draw their attention to their rights under the Distance Selling Regulations, e.g. cancellation rights amongst others."

## 4. PROTECT YOUR COPYRIGHT IN THE WEBSITE CONTENT

"Although you automatically own the copyright in the content that you create, best practice is to remind your visitors! Say, for example, 'Copyright 2011 Lawyers R Great Ltd' and if your logo, designs or name is trademarked, broadcast the fact! After all, you will have spent a lot of money in getting it that far and it will enhance your brand in the market."

## 5. STATE WHO YOU ARE!

"By law you need to state a full postal address and contact number and if you are a limited company, the company's registered address, number and country of registration. This also applies to your emails, so add these details to your signature."

# YOUR WEB CONTENT

When it comes to showing off your products on your site, the same advice applies as on platform sites: you need get pricing, photography and customer service just right.

In addition to this, you can build your online presence around compelling written and visual content to draw in browsers.

# Blogging

Blogging is an easy way to get online, as you write posts on your topic of choice, upload images and video and become the go-to place for customers looking for your advice/tips/services/products. Search engines love blogs and the more you write, the higher up the search-engine ranks you will go. Writing regularly is likely to lead to a loyal readership and it's an effective way to communicate your news with existing and potential customers.

Two to three posts a week is a good amount and should be manageable.

Your blog should be a mix of news and posts about your business but in creative ways – perhaps ideas of how to use/display/wear your goods – and other inspiration posts that display your expertise in your field, perhaps 'How-to' craft projects, posts on latest trends and so on.

To increase the amount of people reading your blog, get involved in the blogging world! Visit others and comment on posts you like, by engaging with the blogging community and you will find word will start to spread about you and your business. Promote your blog posts on Twitter and Facebook so your followers there are alerted to new content too.

Readers can also add their comments to your entries if you allow them and you can use your blog to answer questions and establish yourself as an expert in your field. It's free and easy to get started. Post on your site or try one of the services below for a standalone site.

- Blogger | **www.blogger.com**

- Typepad | **www.typepad.com**

- WordPress | **www.wordpress.com**

Image libraries for photos you can use in your blogs include:

- Image Source | **www.imagesource.com**

- Photos.com | **www.photos.com**

- Getty Images | **www.gettyimages.com**

- Fotlia | **www.en.fotolia.com**

- Shutterstock | **www.shutterstock.com**

- Morgue File | **www.morguefile.com**

- Dreamstime | **www.dreamstime.com**

- Stockfresh | **www.stockfresh.com**

Search for creative commons licensed images you can use commercially from Flickr at: **www.compfight.com**

# Vlogging

After getting to grips with blogging, why not try your hand at vlogging? This stands for video blogging and is an effective way to interact with customers who want to see you, your products, your studio and other happy customers.

*Vlogging expert, Niamh Guckian (director of Totally Wired), offers tips on how to vlog like a pro . . .*

**66** Vlogging can help you tell people your story, using motion pictures and audio. It could be a demonstration of your skills, an atmosphere piece about the place you go for ideas or an interview with a person who inspires you.

## THE GEAR

It's important to get to know your gear – whether using your phone or a fancy-cam, become an expert on your chosen camera.

Where possible use manual control with your camera – this applies to white balance, exposure and focus. Learn the rules and then have fun breaking them.

Use focus and depth of field to add style to your shooting. Using a tripod sets your work apart from amateur shooting and allows for good steady shot composition.

## SAFETY

Using a small camera can make you feel like you can take risks that you wouldn't otherwise. This has advantages at times but don't take unnecessary risks. Don't shoot from rooftops or get into water!

## LIGHT

As a video-blogger, you will mostly be working with available or natural light. Try to get the most from what's available at the time.

## SOUND

Audio recording is a specialist art form. What we need to achieve as self-shooters is clean and non-distorted sound. Distorted audio is not fixable, and can usually be prevented.

## INTERVIEWS

If your piece is interview-based, engage with the contributor, communicate with them and let them know clearly what you want them to do. Create an atmosphere where the contributor is comfortable, and make sure they know they can stop and start again, or ask questions.

Make sure the interview is a sequence, that it has a beginning, middle and end, and can stand alone if necessary.

As with content for your blog, you can vlog about anything you like! Think about what people will find interesting to watch – perhaps that's how you put together a certain item, where certain fabrics come from or an interview with an expert in the field. Make sure your vlog is interesting and informative and people will tune in!

# MAKING MONEY FROM YOUR SITE

## E-commerce tools

Open your website up to sales by adding a shopping cart or plugging in an e-commerce tool. Here are some suggestions.

### SHOPPING CARTS

Add a shopping cart to make life easy for your visitors to click and buy. Check out the shopping cart providers below . . .

- GroovyCart | **www.groovycart.co.uk**

- Zen Cart | **www.zen-cart.com**

- RomanCart | **www.romancart.com**

- osCommerce | **www.oscommerce.com**

- CubeCart | **www.cubecart.com**

- Frooition | **www.frooition.com** (shopping cart and full website)

Research the product that suits you best, taking into account hosting provision, back-end admin, and built-in search engine optimisation.

If you are blogging and want to start selling, consider these plug-in tools as well . . .

- WordPress e-Commerce shopping cart – "suitable for selling your products, services, and or fees online" | **bit.ly/fEgQHo**

- PayPal Shortcodes – insert PayPal buttons in your posts or pages using a shortcode | **wordpress.org/extend/plugins/paypal-shortcodes**

- View a complete list of WordPress e-commerce plugins | **bit.ly/eTEkwZ**

Many e-commerce platform sites come with an in-built payment system. Here are the main ones.

## PAYPAL

Regarded as the leading international payment platform, PayPal (**www.paypal.com/uk**) has more than 84 million active registered accounts and is available in 190 markets, meaning you can successfully trade in all these markets!

For online store owners, PayPal is easy to introduce and offers customers peace of mind that payment will be secure.

The company offers three main products: website payments standard, website payments pro and express checkout. To enable your customers to buy multiple items, use a free PayPal shopping cart. To put the 'Add to Cart' button on your website you can simply copy and paste from PayPal to the coding of your own site. Your customers then click the button to make a purchase.

• Add PayPal button | **bit.ly/blxrUn**

With PayPal, there are no set-up charges, monthly fees or cancellation charges, and fee levels vary depending on the volume of sales.

## GOOGLE WALLET

Google wallet (**www.google.co.uk/wallet**) is a global payment system. There are no set-up charges and fees depend on the volume of your sales. With monthly sales of less than £1,500, the fee is currently 3.4% plus 20p per transaction. This transaction fee decreases in line with sales volumes increasing.

## SAGE PAY

Sage Pay (**www.sagepay.com**) is a card payment service that allows you to accept payments by PayPal and major debit and credit cards. It is simple to manage and easy to integrate within your website. The fee is £20 per month for merchants processing up to 1,000 transactions per quarter and 10p per transaction for merchants processing more than 1,000 transactions per quarter, with a minimum charge of £20 per month. There are no set-up fees, no percentage fees and no annual charges.

TIP { Just-in-time payment

Adding a PayPal payment button to your site will enable you to accept payment from all major credit and debit cards, as well as bank accounts around the world. You can set it up in less than 15 minutes.

# 10 ways to monetise your website

As traffic to your online home increases, so also do your chances of generating income. Make a profit from your content with these top techniques . . .

## 1. SELL ADVERTISING

Offer advertising on your site. The more niche your audience, the more likely you are to attract advertisers.

The information you'll need to provide includes:

- number of unique visitors

- number of impressions

- average duration of visit

- visitor demographics.

Write a basic rate card, add it to your site and send it to corporate marketing departments and media-buying agencies.

The purpose of a media rate card is to show potential advertisers what your site can deliver to them in terms of traffic and possible sales. To do this, include some key points:

- **A brief description of the site:** What it does and for whom.

- **Visitor demographics:** Do you have data on the age of your site visitors, their home region, gender, etc? If so, include it, as it helps build a picture of your audience.

- **Site traffic:** What are your unique visitor numbers and length of time spent on the site? Include a note or graph if the figures are increasing.

- **Costings:** Do you have a cost-per-click (CPC) or cost-per-impression (CPM) rate? If so, include it here, along with the price of other sponsorship options. Offer a menu but leave some flexibility, with 'costed on a project basis' for sponsor features that would benefit from a more tailored proposal.

- **Screenshots:** Showing how and where adverts or sponsored features appear on the site.

- **Media activity:** Note where you've recently been covered in the media, online and off, so that potential sponsors can see how and where you're promoting the site.

- **Testimonials:** Positive comments from existing sponsors give credibility to you and confidence to the next potential sponsor.

- **Team details:** Who are the faces behind the site and what are their credentials? In other words, your background career and activities, etc.

Round this off with your contact details so that anyone interested can get in touch and place an order!

## 2. GOOGLE ADSENSE

Google AdSense (**www.google.co.uk/adsense**) does the work for you: it places relevant ads on your site and earns you money when people click on them. You can customise the appearance of the ads so they sit well with the style of your site.

## 3. TEXTLINKADS

These ads offer direct click-throughs from text on your site. You submit your site to TextLinkAds (**www.text-link-ads.com**) and then upload the ad code provided. It's your choice whether you approve or deny the supplied ads. Once that's done, you start making money as visitors click on the ads. Try this and Skimlinks (**www.skimlinks.com**), which converts words on your site to affiliate links so that you earn from those too.

## 4. SPONSORED CONVERSATIONS

Get paid for posts (and now tweets) with services like IZEA (**www.izea.com**) that match bloggers with advertisers. Some doubt the ethical stance of paying a blogger to write something about a product but there's no doubt that it's a money maker.

## 5. AFFILIATE SCHEMES

Sign up to affiliate schemes like the Amazon Associates programme (**affiliate-program.amazon.co.uk**), where you can earn up to 10% in referrals by linking to Amazon products. The programme works by driving traffic to Amazon through specially formatted links. You earn referral fees on sales generated through those links. Monthly cheques are sent to you from Amazon (when you earn over a certain amount) and it's easy and free to join.

## 6. SPONSORED FEATURES

This could include a host of options. Approach advertisers with suggestions of a sponsored eBook, e-news, podcast, webchat, demonstrations or survey. These applications can be added to your site at a low cost yet generate good revenue. For:

- eBook creation, try **www.blurb.com**

- a survey or poll feature, try **www.surveymonkey.com**

- email marketing, try **www.mailchimp.com**

## 7. EXPERT HELP

Offer your expertise and charge people to log on and watch or listen. This could be made available through:

- Teleclasses: Invite customers and contacts to a call where you offer your expertise on a one-to-many basis.

- GoToWebinar: Deliver a presentation to potentially thousands of paying customers via **www.gotowebinar.co.uk**.

## 8. DEALS WITH SUPPLIERS

Do deals with suppliers. Hosting a design blog? Agree a percentage each time an order is made via your site. Hosting a shed-working blog? Create a directory that includes all garden office suppliers but with an enhanced listing for those who pay.

## 9. TURN A BLOG INTO A BOOK

Follow the lead of Debbie O'Connor who turned the content of her blog, Motivating Mum (**www.motivatingmum.co.uk**), into a book called *Motivating Business Mums*. It's now selling across the UK and acting as an effective marketing tool for the site!

## 10. PLEASE DONATE

If you'd rather just ask for a small donation from your visitors, this is possible too via a donate feature from PayPal. Add a PayPal donate button to your site: **tinyurl.com/63swy9x**

## TIP { PitchUp!

Apply to StartUp Britain's PitchUp project to have your products placed in front of national buyers. Shortlisted contenders get the opportunity to meet with retailers such as John Lewis and be in with a chance of securing a contract.

# BEAUTIFUL BUSINESS:
# CAROLA VAN DYKE

**Name:** Carola van Dyke

**Business:** Carola van Dyke Ltd.

**Website:** www.carolavandyke.co.uk | www.tinytulips.co.uk

Carola van Dyke started her textile business Tiny Tulips 12 years ago, designing quirky children's wear.

"I made clothes for my own children, and was stopped in the street quite often to find out where I had bought them. This moved on to taking individual commissions and a few months later supplying the designer children's shop in Brighton where we lived at the time."

For several years, Carola ran the business on a smallish scale, supplying products to shops around the UK, as well as being a full-time mum.

"With the children getting older and going to school, I was driven by creative new ideas, and expanded into soft furnishings with my new business Carola van Dyke Ltd. My style and trademark for this originated from having access to only small scraps of vintage and continental fabrics leftover from Tiny Tulips collections. I wanted to combine my paintings and textiles, create pictures, treating the off-cuts like a painter uses a palette. I started creating individual cushions with appliquéd flowers, birds, country animals and dogs."

Carola takes inspiration from her surroundings:

"Living in the countryside at the foot of the South Downs influences my colours, textures and subjects; my designs are carefree, and bring across my love for colour. My aim is that they should create a sense of adventure and fun, while comfort and quality are essential too."

Her big breakthrough came after she took part in tradeshow Pulse in London in 2011. She had planned to take mostly baby booties with her, but at the last minute decided to take along some of the new cushions she had designed.

"The turning point came when Mary Portas visited my stand – she pointed at the dog cushions and asked for a card. Two weeks later, I got home to find a man had left a message on my answer machine, but his name and number were unintelligible! Thank goodness they called back a few days later, and it turned out to be House of Fraser where Mary Portas would have her shop."

Initially, Carola received an order for 60 cushions and then two weeks later a further order for 200! "The cushions then appeared in her TV programme, and in lots of interior magazines – I just was so lucky that the decision was made to use my cushions for advertising her new shop."

In order to promote the business, Carola takes part in one trade show a year and also finds that press mentions are a powerful way to let people know about her business.

"I've worked very hard this year on getting features in magazines, cushions on shop pages and so on. Good lifestyle photos and some cutouts are a must, and it's important to try to find the right people with the right magazines."

From Mary Portas taking her cushions, Carola found that the business grew and grew.

"The PR with Mary Portas' name attached to it changed the speed the orders came in, and therefore the time I had for making the cushions. With all the publicity the cushions received, people were on their way to House of Fraser to buy their favoured dog cushion, or directly from me online. At this point, I was still very much a one-woman business, making everything myself!"

With each cushion taking over two hours to make, Carole realised she could only make five to six cushions a day, which wouldn't be enough to fulfill her orders.

"There was a month of confusion and slight panic on our side: should we go to a factory, either in the UK or abroad, start our own factory, train a number of home machinists, or sell the designs? That month was quite emotional too, as I was so worried that the whole thing would slip through my fingers; there wasn't enough time for me to make them myself, but equally there wasn't enough time for me to train other people either. I just couldn't see how my individual, sometimes on-the-spot made-up product, could be 'mass' produced, in a way that I would still agree with the quality and the price."

However, all the stockists were understanding. Carola worked out small, weekly deliveries to everybody, with newly trained machinists and her husband working as 'head cutter' and cutting endless panels, animal pieces and backings!

"It took a month to run properly, but at the end we could do around 100 cushions a week."

Carola still designs all of the products herself – "I have such a strong idea of what the end product has to look like, and it will be impossible to explain that to other people!" She has, however, taken on six members of staff who help her produce the items, which are now sold in the USA, Australia and Ireland.

"I think the easiest way to go global is doing trade shows abroad, or having a bit of luck if they come over and see a product at a trade show here. If you are exhibiting in a different country, it is very important to look into its customs a bit, so you have an idea about how to approach things. A bit of knowledge of the country and the people doesn't hurt."

Carola is keen to build a stronger, more recognisable brand in 2013. She intends to look in more detail at expanding the business by getting her products sold in department stores, boutiques, garden centres and museums. She also has lots of ideas for new products as well as new designs.

"Last year, my new idea was the fabric trophy heads! We are also currently working with an exciting British ceramics company to produce plates, mugs etc with the textile images. These should come out in September 2013. I also want to develop our manufacturing and logistics, whilst remaining true to the ethos of the brand, and our passion for British craftsmanship – these things are very important to me as I grow my business."

# Top tips!

1. "Set up a business that you truly believe in, that you understand and have a passion for."

2. "Be different than the others who are offering a similar product or service."

3. "Plan your business, with either weekly or monthly goals, but be realistic in what you can achieve in a certain time."

4. "Although you must know your business inside out, you must be able to delegate – don't think that you are the only person who can possibly do a certain job in your business very well. If you want to expand you need to let go of one-person control and start trusting the people you will employ. Once you've worked out how to delegate well, there is suddenly a lot of space in your head and in the week for new ideas."

# Chapter Ten

## MARKETING I.
# PR AND
## TRADE SHOWS

Sales are coming in and you want to tell the world about you and your new business. Profile brings new customers, new sales and headlines!

# GETTING KNOWN

Become known in the press and online by making friends with the media, hosting events, entering awards and becoming an expert in your field. Create the right first impression, whether a customer meets you at an event or visits your site. Here's guidance on how to achieve it all. First step: getting known.

## PLOT THE SCRIPT

Your business needs a narrative. You should have heard of the 'elevator pitch' – a one or two-sentence summary of exactly what your business does, adapted to the brevity of the average journey in a lift with an executive or other Big Cheese who can help your enterprise.

You need the same for the *story* of your business. This is not just a question of what your business does – but why it is doing it. Where it's come from; where it's going; what it's all about. The atmosphere you want to convey. It should direct all your marketing efforts.

Imagine your business as the star of its own Hollywood movie. Is it an action hero, battling against the odds (think James Dyson) or a brand-leading lady (think Cath Kidston)? Plot the action and write the script. It will help you define your message to the media.

## FIND THE RIGHT CONTACTS

Next, research the journalists you think are interested in your field. Note their email addresses from the bottom of their articles, follow them on Twitter, get to know them and send them exclusive stories about you and your business.

## FOLLOWING THE MEDIA

Follow media contacts and channels on Twitter to pick up on profile opportunities. Here are a few from radio/TV/magazines:

- @BBCBreakfast
- @talktothepress
- @findaTVexpert
- @TheSTStyle
- @lifeandstyle
- @countrylivingUK
- @PrimaMag
- @HB
- @TelegraphMag
- @StellaMagazine

Please contact Enterprise Nation with your story. We are always profiling start-ups and small businesses on our website, in books (like this one!), in kits, in videos and as part of the national StartUp Britain campaign.

Submit your story at **www.enterprisenation.com**.

# Write a press release

Writing a press release costs nothing but your time, yet it can generate thousands of pounds worth of publicity. If you're emailing a press release to journalists, write the text in the body of the email and include it in an attachment, too.

Your press release should have an attention-grabbing headline, the main facts in the first sentence and evidence and quotes from as high-profile people and companies as possible in the main body of the text. Include great quality images wherever you can to lift the piece and put a face to the brand (but don't make the email file size huge!). You could also use a press-release distribution service to secure wider exposure. My personal favourite is ResponseSource (**www.response source.com**) but there's also PR Newswire (**www.prnewswire.co.uk**) and PRWeb (**www.prweb.com**). If you don't get a response, follow up!

Sometimes journalists are simply looking for suitable products for a shopping page or a photoshoot so images are important. It is worth embedding a good range of small pictures in your email and letting them know that you can supply high-resolution images on request.

Be prepared to offer product loans to publications as well – often magazine stylists need items to use in photoshoots, and sometimes need them urgently so be ready to send these out quickly. This is a great way to get extra publicity as they will credit the use of your item in the feature.

You can ask the journalist for a PDF of the feature after publication and add it to your press page on your website or post on your social media channels to 'show off' how your products have been featured.

Blogs and online magazines are now just as highly regarded as print publications so make sure you build up a contact list for these as well. Make sure to only contact ones which are relevant to your field. They will usually link directly to your website – invaluable for those spontaneous sales and SEO efficiency.

## NINE COMPONENTS OF A SUCCESSFUL PRESS RELEASE

1. Attention-grabbing headline.

2. The first line is punchy and explains the what, who, why and where of the headline.

3. Back up the headline and intro with more detail – facts and figures if you have them.

4. Include a quote from you (or your business partner, if relevant)

5. Can you include a quote from someone else? A happy customer, industry expert or celebrity?

6. End with a call to action. Where can people go to find out more/how to download the report/which site to visit to claim a free gift, etc.?

7. Include 'Notes to Editors', with brief details on you and your company.

8. Remember to include contact details – your email address and telephone number.

9. Attach a relevant and interesting image.

### TIP { Link request

If you're being featured online ask the journalist if they can include a live link to your site. That way, readers can be on your site within a click.

# 12 ways to kick-start your business's PR

*Greg Simpson, founder and director of Press for Attention (**www.pressforattention.com**) gives his top 12 tips for building a successful PR campaign . . .*

### 1. HAVE A 'CUNNING PLAN'

 Too many people rush into PR and marketing campaigns with no real plan. Ask yourself:

• What are the goals of the campaign?

• How do you want to come across in terms of tone?

• Key messages – what do you want to get across?

## 2. CONSIDER HOW VARIOUS COMPANIES GET THEIR MESSAGES ACROSS

Tactics include PR stunts, press releases, controversy, photo opportunities, comment/opinion pieces, debates, flash mobs, press trips, celebrity endorsements, competitions. There are so many ways to get noticed. Blend them to your requirements and skills.

## 3. RESEARCH YOUR CUSTOMER/AUDIENCE

There is little point getting a full article page in *Dog Grooming Monthly* if you sell organic ice-cream to boutique hotels! Find out who your ideal customer is and research what they read, listen to and watch. Then, *really* take the time to read the publications and get to know what sort of stories they publish.

## 4. FIND THE NEWS HOOK

Be honest, is your story really news?

Examples include: new products, new staff, new promotions, new premises, anniversaries, company expansion, financial milestones and charity efforts.

You can also provide topical comment on a newsworthy subject. Keep an eye out for issues that affect your business or your customers. This takes practice and you need to establish credibility in your subject area first. Consider starting a blog that provides regular, lively and informed comment in your area of expertise to build your profile.

## 5. GOT A STORY?

Great! Now you need a *simple* press release for a journalist to refer to. People worry that their efforts don't sound flashy enough to warrant attention but you aren't aiming for a Booker Prize, you are aiming for coherent and interesting *news*.

Use 'Who, What, When, How and Why?' as a framework and imagine yourself as the journalist. Is this definitely of interest to their readers? Is it simple enough to understand? Does it stand up on its own?

I would stick to a maximum of 300 words and keep the press release focused on the news angle.

## 6. HIT THEM BETWEEN THE EYES

Journalists get hundreds of press releases every day. Ensure that the headline and first paragraph sum up the entire story in a nutshell. Ideally, your press release should still make sense even if an editor drops two or three paragraphs.

I call the journalist beforehand to outline my story. This helps iron out any creases and demonstrates that you are trying to work with them and their audience.

## 7. DON'T BE TEMPTED TO START HASSLING

I very rarely 'chase' a journalist once I have sent a press release. If it is good enough, they will use it. Hassling will not push it to the top of the pile and may see it heading towards the recycle bin. Be patient and able to help if the journalist does come back. Don't go on holiday the day after you have sent a story out!

## 8. PHOTOS – THINK IN PICTURES

Consider what makes you read a story when you flick through a newspaper. Headlines play their part but the impact of an interesting picture is greater still. People 'sell' stories, so ensure that anyone in your shot is clearly visible and captioned. Try to show the impact of the news – product shots are okay but a product in the hands of a customer is better.

## 9. BUILD A RELATIONSHIP

PR is not a them vs. us war with journalists, it is a working relationship where both parties stand to gain. They get news/insight and you get free publicity in exchange for a fresh take on things or for your role in illustrating the impact of an issue with greater clarity.

## 10. MEASURE AND EVALUATE

How do you know if your gym regime and new diet is working? You get on the scales (peeking from between your fingers). Are you getting through to the right journalists? How many stories are you sending out? How many are getting coverage? How much coverage do they get? Do your pictures and even your key messages get included? Are you being invited to comment on topical issues?

### 11. PUT YOUR PR HAT ON AND EXECUTE THE PLAN

I know many small businesses that freeze when it comes to actually putting their plans into action. Schedule and commit to some time every week to do something that contributes to your PR campaign.

### 12. A FINAL TIP

PR agencies spend vast amounts on media monitoring software for mentions of their clients or to keep in touch with specific debates. You can do a lot of it for free. Have a play with Google Alerts (**www.google.com/alerts**).

# Write articles

If you are a talented writer, another good idea is to consider offering to write articles for magazines in your specific field. You may or may not get paid for this, but either way they will usually include a link to your website which is extra exposure. The online magazine world is burgeoning and the magazines are often niche so find ones suitable to you and get in touch about contributing.

• For interiors, vintage and crafts, *91 Magazine* | **www.91magazine.co.uk**

• For weddings, *Reverie Magazine* | **www.reveriemag.com**

• For surface pattern design, *MOYO magazine* | **www.issuu.com/moyomagazine**

# Enter awards

Enter awards and competitions and enjoy the press coverage that goes with it. Many award schemes are free to enter and targeted at start-up businesses. Writing the entry will help to clarify your goals and vision, and winning will bring profile and prizes. Check out the following:

- *Country Living* Magazine Kitchen Table Talent Awards (**www.allaboutyou.com/countryliving**) – if you're working on a talent or skill from the kitchen table and know it can be turned into a business, this competition is for you. Prizes include office equipment, profile in the magazine and advice/support from business experts!

- Shell LiveWIRE Grand Ideas Awards (**www.shell-livewire.org/awards**) – up to six awards per month of £1,000 for anyone aged 16 to 30 looking to get an idea off the ground.

- The Pitch (**www.thepitchuk.com**) – enter regional heats and pitch to experienced judges for a place in the national finals. Takes place across the UK.

- Social Enterprise Awards (**www.socialenterprise.org.uk/events**) – celebrates social enterprises of all ages.

- Nectar Small Business Awards (**www.nectar.com/business-sba2012**) – offers cash prizes and plenty of Nectar points!

- Startups Awards (**www.startupsawards.co.uk**) – celebrating small businesses of all shapes and sizes.

One way to attract profile and attention is to have a celebrity endorse your product or service. Lyndsey Young has seen the benefit of this. She is the inventor of Count On It food freshness labels and she secured an endorsement from celebrity mum and actress Amanda Holden, who has used the labels when preparing meals for her daughter. This support has been beneficial in leading to other marketing successes, including features in *BBC Easy Cook*, *Your Homes*, *That's Life*, *Cook Vegetarian* and *Healthy* magazine.

# Join a group or club

Signing up to a local business club or network is good for business and your social life. You get together to do deals but also end up making friends. Check out these national business networks to find your natural fit:

- 1230 TWC (**www.1230.co.uk**) – events for women in business

- 4Networking (**www.4networking.biz**) – national network of business breakfast groups

- The Athena Network (**www.theathenanetwork.com**) – networking organisation for women in business

- Business Scene (**www.business-scene.com**) – hosts regional and national networking events as well as hosting an online directory of over 10,000 events across the UK

- Jelly (**www.uk-jelly.org.uk**) – an American import which encourages casual gatherings of co-workers, with events held in people's homes, the local coffee shop or workspaces. The idea is that you meet in relaxed surroundings and creative ideas are stimulated by the experience. There are now Jelly events taking place in all corners of the UK.

- School for Creative Startups (**www.schoolforcreativestartups.com**) – headed by serial entrepreneur Doug Richard, School for Startups travels the UK hosting events for anyone considering starting a business. Gems from Doug's presentations are broadcast via S4STV.

- Women in Rural Enterprise (WiRE) (**www.wireuk.org**) – networking and business club for rural women in business

- StartUp Saturday (**www.enterprisenation.com/events/startupsaturday**) – A weekly class hosted by Enterprise Nation that not only offers instruction on how to start a business but also ensures a ready-made support group for anyone wishing to become their own boss.

- Enterprise Nation (**www.enterprisenation.com**) – EN also offers a national membership which entitles you to discounts and offers, free monthly eBooks and the opportunity to come together with peers at local networking events or at national conferences.

From attending events and being part of a national network, you may meet businesses with whom there is a shared opportunity.

# ATTEND TRADE SHOWS

Promote your brand by attending the shows your customers attend. Craft fairs and shows are excellent places to sell products, meet customers and get your business in front of the ideal target audience.

- Start by deciding on the type of craft fair you want to exhibit at, i.e. where your customers are likely to be. Then look at location – is the fair out of town, meaning hotel and transport costs and, if so, are there ways you could reduce your expenditure, for example staying with friends, or sharing costs with another business?

- Carry out online searches and talk to other crafters to find out the best fairs to attend and keep updated with crafting/interiors blogs and websites for mention of the more popular events. Don't forget your local shops and newsletters/magazines as these are often a source of useful information.

- Confident you've found the right fair, look at how much exhibition space you'll need and can afford. Look carefully at what is included in the price – will they provide a table and chairs, electricity, an internet connection? Most events will have an online or paper application process; be clear about what you do, make and sell – the organisers may have thousands of people applying for space so make their decision as easy as possible. Once happy with your application form, press send and wait! It may take a couple of days before you receive confirmation.

## Merchandise must-dos

If you have been accepted for the fair, congratulations! There will be lots to do to get you ready to exhibit so here are some key points to start with:

- Make a list of what you have in stock – do you have enough of each product to take with you, or will you need to produce some extra stock? How will you price these items, and will you be displaying prices on them, or will you have a clear price list which people can refer to?

- Your exhibition space will need to be decorated – think about sourcing items and backdrops that will highlight your brand and your message, and show off products to their best advantage. For example, do you sell handmade rings? Instead of having them laid flat in a box, could you display them on a hand mannequin or use a prop to dangle them from? If you sell clothing, do you need to take a mirror? These little things can make the difference between someone buying your product or walking away. Think about stalls you have visited when you've been at craft fairs and the ones that stood out to you – can you take inspiration from them to create your own stand?

- Don't forget marketing materials, such as business cards, flyers and special offer leaflets. Do you have these ready or will you need to produce them? Do you have anything you can use as a handout to passers-by?

- Packaging materials – you will need to ensure you have enough of this to last you for the entire fair. If you wrap your products up, it could be a nice idea to invest in some stickers with your logo and website details to seal the package, so that when the customer gets home they remember you and may be tempted to buy again. You could even look at customised carrier bags – extra advertising as your customers wander around the fair.

- Ahead of the event, ask organisers how the drop-off and delivery process works so you have enough time to set up your stall and get yourself ready before customers begin to arrive and you're out of the venue by the correct time once the event finishes.

- Consider whether you need public liability insurance to display your products.

# The art of networking

Trade shows are also an excellent opportunity for networking, a vital tool for growing your business and something that can bring you all sorts of unexpected opportunities. Here are some must-dos for successful networking:

- Wear your name tag (if you have one) on your right side. It's easy to catch sight of when you are shaking hands.

- Deliver a nice firm handshake and make eye contact.

- Say your name clearly and, in under ten seconds, tell the other person who you are and what you do.

- Listen carefully. Ask the other person plenty of questions about their line of business, their family, their hobbies, without being too intrusive or personal.

- Be positive and energetic.

- Swap business cards.

- Send a 'thank you' email after the event, confirming any actions you and they have promised.

- Keep in regular, and meaningful, contact.

# BEAUTIFUL BUSINESS:
# KATE SCHURICHT CERAMICS

**Name:** Kate Schuricht

**Business:** Kate Schuricht Ceramics

**Website:** www.kateschuricht.com

**Social media:** www.seekandadore.com/kateschuricht

Kate Schuricht always knew that she wanted to be an artist, and after studying three-dimensional design (wood, metal, ceramics and plastics) at Brighton University from 1993–6 and attending an International Ceramic residency in Japan for the summer of 1996, she was determined to have her own ceramic studio in London.

> "After seeing the potters in Japan who combined their love of clay with their lifestyle in artistic communities, I was really set on having my own studio and set up at Cockpit Arts in Holborn within weeks of returning from Japan. To start with, I worked part-time at the Crafts Council and spent evenings and weekends in my studio, sharing the space with a fellow potter friend."

Kate's first pieces were sold at her degree show and then at a New Designers exhibition, but Kate credits her first big break to press at the Cockpit Open Studios.

> "Within months I had been featured in several different glossy interiors magazines starting with *The World Of Interiors*, *Country Living*, *Homes and Interiors* and then *Elle Decoration*. As a result, my raku and stoneware ceramics were also seen by interior designers and architects and interest grew amongst gallery owners, design stores and museums."

From there, Kate grew the business steadily by exhibiting at specialist ceramic exhibitions around the country as well as mixed craft shows, Open Studios, regional and international galleries. Her website is a good source of publicity as is the online selling site for craftspeople called 'Seek and Adore' (**www.seekandadore.com**), where she can blog and give more information about her products.

> "Over the years, I have had my work featured in several books and ceramic magazines. This year I have also written a book/catalogue. And I have produced a colour brochure explaining more about the ideas behind the pieces and the specialist processes used in making them."

Kate believes that her business has been a success due to getting out there, visiting and forming good relationships with appropriate galleries, training work experience students and studio assistants, as well as teaching her craft and applying for collaborative projects. Although she mostly works alone, she has recently trained a freelance studio assistant who provides essential help at busy times of the year.

"All the pieces are entirely handmade in my studio and are glazed and fired on site, so sometimes help is needed."

As for the next 12 months, Kate has plans to build her presence in European and international markets, but would still like to keep her company relatively small.

"I don't have a product range or production method that lends itself to mass production and my market is quite specialist: collectors, architects/interior designers, museums and galleries. So I have no intention of my company growing really big. However, I am planning to develop some new work and produce larger pieces in 2013 which are more one-off or limited editions, as well as small scale installations."

# Top tips!

- "It's important to immerse yourself in the field in which you are thinking of starting your business and become something of an expert. Visit all the shows, understand the price points, the marketplace for your product or service and the way that things operate. Ask lots of questions, research similar companies on the internet, ask colleagues' advice and look for a business mentor. Look for gaps in the market or a unique angle on things that makes your product or service really noticeable and special."

- "Think of the way that your business will fit in with your lifestyle – that can always be a make or break element. It is hard work to grow and build your own business but it could easily be the most rewarding project you have taken on."

- "I think it is essential to draw on a creative skill or area of your craft that you feel truly passionate about. After all, your enthusiasm and genuine interest in what you do is infectious to others and is an important part of your business identity."

TIP { A fair difference

Fairs are generally about selling your products directly to the public, whereas trade shows are generally for trade only, where suppliers take wholesale orders and no direct retail purchases take place. You can of course exhibit at both, depending on whether you wish to sell to trade customers as well as the general public.

# Useful links and resources

- *Country Living* Spring and Christmas Fairs | **www.countrylivingfair.com**, **@CLFairs**
- *House Beautiful* events and directory | **www.ukhandmade.co.uk/events**, **www.ukhandmade.co.uk/shopdirectory**, **www.ukhandmade.co.uk/localgroups**, **@ukhandmade**
- Suffolk Craft Society | **www.suffolkcraftsociety.org**
- Glasgow Craft Mafia | **www.glasgowcraftmafia.com**
- Birmingham Craft Mafia | **www.birminghamcraftmafia.com**
- Stitch & Craft Show | **www.stitchandcraft.co.uk**
- Farmers' markets | **www.farmersmarkets.net**
- London Farmers' Markets | **www.lfm.org.uk**
- British Sellers on Etsy | **britishemporia.blogspot.co.uk**
- Crafty Fox Market | **craftyfoxmarket.blogspot.com**
- Craft Fair Advice on Folksy | **blog.folksy.com/category/seller-tips/craft-fair-advice**
- Art and craft events in Lincolnshire | **www.tempopromotes.co.uk**
- Selvedge fairs | **www.selvedge.org/fair**
- Pick 'n' Mix Makers Market, Norfolk | **picknmixmakersmarket.blogspot.com**
- Craft Guerilla, East London | **www.craftguerrilla.com**

- Crafts Council | **www.craftscouncil.org.uk**
- *Crafts* Magazine | **www.craftscouncil.org.uk/crafts-magazine**
- National directory resource for contemporary craft | **www.craftscouncil.org.uk/craft-directory**
- Listing of creative courses | **www.frombritainwithlove.com/directory/creative-courses**
- Craft Reactor, Edinburgh | **www.craftreactor.com**

# BECOME AN EXPERT

Set yourself up as an expert in your field and the media will come knocking on your door. Do this by writing a book, offering training or developing your own app! Here are some ways in which you can promote your expertise.

## 1. PUBLISH A BOOK

Become a published author on the topic of your choice by self-publishing via sites such as Lulu, Blurb and Ubyu. Utilise the book as a business development tool, printing on demand to take copies to events, and offering free and downloadable versions to potential customers. Being an author gives you credibility and gives customers information and insight.

- Blurb | **www.blurb.com**
- Lulu | **www.lulu.com**
- Ubyu | **www.ubyubooks.com**
- Contact Brightword Publishing (the publishers of this book) with your book idea | **www.enterprisenation.com**

## 2. PRESENT YOURSELF

Put yourself forward to speak or demonstrate at events (consider asking for a fee and/or costs to be covered) or suggest being a satellite speaker, where you are beamed into the conference hall via video link-up, so saving the effort and expense of travel. Invite customers and prospects and make the presentation openly available via SlideShare (**www.slideshare.com**).

## 3. HOST A WEBINAR

Share your expertise or demonstrate a process by hosting a webinar or visual presentation where a 'live' audience can see you and interact. Achieve this via platforms such as GoToMeeting (**www.gotomeeting.com**), GoToWebinar (**www.gotowebinar.com**), WebEx (**www.webex.co.uk**) and Salesforce (**www.salesforce.com**), and remember to host it at a time that suits your target audience.

## 4. PRODUCE A FILM

Maybe the word 'film' is a little ambitious but you can create your own video content with an affordable camcorder or smartphone, or by hiring in a cameraman and having a sponsored series of guides that can be uploaded to video-sharing sites such as YouTube (**www.youtube.com**), Vimeo (**www.vimeo.com**) and eHow (**www.ehow.co.uk**), and easily embedded into your site.

You could always collaborate with another creative company on a video. That way, both of you gain fresh content and it will create more coverage for both parties as they distribute it amongst both their sets of followers, customers and so on.

## 5. BROADCAST A PODCAST

For customers who like to listen to what you have to say at a time that suits them, upload a podcast with top tips, interviews and your thoughts of the day. Make it available on your site, iTunes and Podcast Alley to be sure of a wide audience. Follow advice from podcast producer San Sharma on how to record a podcast on a Skype call.

- Submit a podcast to the iTunes store | **www.apple.com/itunes/podcasts/specs.html**
- Podcast Alley | **www.podcastalley.com**

*You can produce a podcast interview using Skype, Pamela Call Recorder, and a little editing know-how. San Sharma (online community manager at Enterprise Nation (**www.enterprisenation.com**) shows how it's done, in five simple steps . . .*

1. Sign up for a free Skype account (**www.skype.com**) and download the Skype software.

2. If you're using a Windows machine, download Pamela Call Recorder (**www.pamela.biz**), which lets you record your Skype calls. If you're on a Mac, you can download Call Recorder for Skype (**www.ecamm.com**). Both have free trial versions, but only cost around £13 when that's expired.

3. Call up your interviewee using Skype. If they're a Skype user, too, that will be a free call but if they're on a fixed or mobile line, you'll need to get some Skype Credit (**bit.ly/epymNm**).

4. Once you've made a connection and agreed with the interviewee the format of the conversation, hit the record button on your call recorder software and you're off!

5. Edit using Audacity (**audacity.sourceforge.net**), which is free for Windows and Macs, or with GarageBand (**www.apple.com/ilife/garageband**), which comes with most Macs (you can also buy it on the App Store).

And the easiest way to share your recording is by uploading it to Audioboo (**www.audioboo.com**), which lets people listen to it on the web, embedded on your website, via iTunes or on a mobile phone.

## 6. DELIVER TRAINING

Whether your skill is in reupholstering furniture or developing stylish interior concepts, your knowledge can be shared with others. Rather than seeing this as surrendering intelligence to potential competitors, offer instruction you're comfortable with that will create fans and followers who will learn from you, buy from you and, critically, encourage others to do the same. Check out platforms GoToTraining (**www.gototraining.com**) and WebEx Training (**www.webex.co.uk/products/elearning-and-online-training.html**), encourage contacts to sign up and then after the demonstration you have a chance to follow up with a group of new contacts.

# Price point

These creative options will raise your profile but you can also generate revenue from them. Your options are:

- make your content and knowledge available at no charge to customers, to build your reputation as the go-to person and place for a particular product, service or ideas

- charge for access/downloads/viewing and turn your micropublishing activity into a revenue stream in its own right.

Individual judgement will be needed in this and it's something you can assess over time. Start with a mix of charged-for and free content, ensure you are providing good value and incentives for your community to remain engaged, and the options to introduce charged-for content will increase.

# Chapter Eleven
## MARKETING II.
## ONLINE
## PROMOTION

G ET WELL-KNOWN online and attract customers to your site through search engine optimisation, social tagging and pay-per-click advertising.

# SEO AND ONLINE ADVERTS

## Rise up the search engine ranks

Search engine optimisation, or SEO, is the process by which you can improve rankings for your website in the top search engines such as Google, so that your site appears on the first few pages of results rather than page 75!

Google uses software known as 'spiders' to crawl the web on a regular basis and find sites to add to its index. There are steps you can take to make it easier for the spiders to find and add your site.

### START WITH THE HOMEPAGE

Provide high-quality, text-based content on your pages – especially your homepage. If your homepage has useful information and good quality, relevant text, it's more likely to be picked up by the spiders. Beyond the homepage, write pages that clearly describe your topic/service/product. Think about the key words users would type to find your pages and include them on the site.

### MAKE CONTRIBUTIONS

Identify influential bloggers and sites in your trade/industry, contact them and offer to write posts. You can also improve your visibility by writing helpful comments in forums and on other people's posts.

## RUN COMPETITIONS

Create a buzz by running competitions. This could be simply to win one of your products or services, or could be more interactive by getting customers to submit something. Perhaps photographs of how they've used your products for example. This could be run through Instagram using a hashtag, and the best photo wins a prize. You could also offer other influential bloggers to run a competition on their blog, to reach out to their readership rather than just your own.

## BE WELL-CONNECTED

Improve the rank of your site by increasing the number of other high-quality sites that link to your pages; these are referred to as 'inbound links'. For example, if you're running a competition, go to sites that promote competitions and add yours.

You can also register your site with the major search engines.

- Google | **www.google.co.uk/addurl**
- Yahoo! | **search.yahoo.com/info/submit.html**
- Bing | **www.bing.com/toolbox/submit-site-url**

Add your domain to local search services such as:

- Google Maps | **www.google.co.uk/maps**
- Qype | **www.qype.co.uk**
- Yahoo! Local | **uk.local.yahoo.com**

## TAGGING

A webpage's title, referred to as a 'title tag', is part of the SEO mix and can make a difference to your search rankings. It is also the text that appears in the top of the browser window. Include in your title tag your company name and the main key phrase you'd like the search engines to associate with your webpage, keeping it between 60 and 90 characters in length. Duncan Green of Moo Marketing is an SEO expert and explains:

"The title tag on the homepage for Moo Marketing reads: 'Moo Marketing – Search Engine Marketing – PPC Management – Search Engine Optimisation'; as you can see, the title element is 85 characters long, contains three key phrases and identifies the subject of the webpage."

# Pay-per-click (PPC) advertising

The results from your efforts in SEO will appear on the main engines (Google, Yahoo! and Bing) in the central column of the page as a natural or 'organic' search result. But have you spotted results on the right of the page when searching for items yourself? These are paid-for results and referred to as pay-per-click or PPC advertising. PPC is where you pay to have ads displayed when people type in certain words, in the hope it will attract more visitors to your site.

Google AdWords (**adwords.google.co.uk**) is such a form of PPC advertising. Think of the key words or phrases you reckon your customers will be searching for and apply them in your Google campaign. Link to your homepage or other pages on the site where you're running a promotion and make the most of geotargeting, which lets you target your ads to specific territories and languages.

You are in full control of the budget and campaign duration.

# Advertising on blogs or online magazines

Many small business owners are unable to afford the advertising rates of the national glossy magazines, but you can increase brand awareness by advertising on blogs which cover your specific target market. If you make crocheted items, look to the craft blogs, or if you make soft furnishings, there are many homes and interiors blogs you could approach.

Online magazines are becoming very popular. Again, many of these are niche and generally offer lower advertising rates than the glossies. These advertisements tend to link straight through to your website and as they are online they have a global readership and can potentially introduce you to an international customer base.

# Spread the word

Make it easy for visitors to spread word of your site through social sharing. Have your site Stumbled, Dugg and Tweeted and make the most of this viral effect. You can add these social book-marking tools by visiting AddThis (**www.addthis.com**) and choosing the icons you'd like to have displayed on your site.

The most popular are:

- Delicious | **www.delicious.com**
- Digg | **www.digg.com**
- StumbleUpon | **www.stumbleupon.com**
- Twitter | **www.twitter.com**

# BEAUTIFUL BUSINESS:
# RACHAEL TAYLOR

**Name:** Rachael Taylor

**Website:** www.rachaeltaylordesigns.co.uk

**Social media:** @rachael_taylor_ | www.rachaeltaylordesigns.blogspot.com

**Online magazine:** www.dowhatyouloveforlife.com/moyo

Designer Rachael Taylor has always worked in the design industry, initially as a print and design technician for a small textile company, then as a surface pattern design specialist for Hallmark UK for a further two years.

> "The experience of working in-house was invaluable and the people were fantastic, however I always felt more of a number than an individual designer. It was also very competitive and I never felt I was being true to me. I always knew I was meant to do something else and I just needed to figure out what that was! I always say my 'inner doodle' was set free once I decided to go it alone."

Before she left full-time employment, Rachael spent time building up her portfolio and setting up meetings with potential clients.

> "In the beginning I took baby steps and set myself weekly goals. It was scary but I knew I really had to go for it."

Although she got a few 'no's' to start with, she persevered.

> "Dealing with rejection can be hard but I'm someone who doesn't like the 'what ifs'. I'd rather try something than to have never given it a chance."

After freelancing for a while, Rachael dreamed of putting her own stamp on products and being able to add her name to collections. After receiving lots of independent bespoke requests, she decided to launch a small product line in the UK.

"Shortly after, I started receiving licensing requests as companies saw the potential that my own individual collections had. I never assumed I'd become an international brand, I just wanted to be recognised as an independent artist but before I knew it I had built a design label."

Rachael's biggest tip for promoting a small business is free social media. She has set up a Facebook page and sends out daily updates to her followers, as well as using Twitter and Pinterest as marketing tools to share links and pictures from her site.

"Setting up a blog and sharing your work is essential marketing, and it is also important to share other designers and artists work too. This helps create a network or community of contacts that may be useful in your career and will drive more attention to your website."

Another avenue that has worked well for Rachael has been to submit her work to other sites that are relevant to her industry.

"I am a surface pattern designer so submitting my work to sites like 'Print and Pattern' (**printpattern.blogspot.co.uk**) has been instrumental in driving more interest to my business and my designs."

Rachael also believes the design of the website has been crucial to her whole branding and launching a successful design business.

"Having a well-managed website is also really important. My site took about a year to plan and build as I wanted a truly bespoke site that reflects my design style and work ethic."

Investing in PR and marketing is also crucial at busy times when she wants to push new designs or collections, and Rachael has invested in a freelance PR consultant who has successfully secured numerous product features in leading design magazines.

Rachael has grown the business by gradually building up a small amount of clients.

"I took each 'yes' and new contract as a sign I was doing the right thing and as each job came in I gained more confidence and courage."

Collaborations have also been a way Rachael has expanded the business, whether that's collaborating with a design licensing partner or setting up a new partnership to create an e-course and magazine.

"Sometimes two heads are better than one. When you're self-employed (particularly in the beginning) you have various roles to juggle such as PR, marketing, accounting and so on. So it's important to recognise when you need help. Investing in staff can be scary but without it I didn't get any design time. That alone set off alarm bells and I knew something had to change."

Rachael has hired a studio assistant and a freelance PR consultant as well as a bookkeeper and a chartered accountant. She has launched her new online store with the help of a web designer.

"I also work with two fantastic photographers, and with my joint ventures 'The Art and Business of Surface Pattern Design' and 'MOYO Magazine' I work alongside my business partner and a project manager."

Rachael has already received global success, particularly in the USA, and recently signed with the Lilla Rogers studio.

"Lilla is now my amazing international agent and this will hopefully help me have more time to focus on designing."

# Top tips!

1. "Believe in yourself, take that leap! I always think if you want something enough, you really can make it happen. I made a promise to myself to stay truly dedicated to my goal (and never, *ever* give up!)"

2. "Daily, weekly and monthly goals are realistic and manageable. Remember to celebrate your achievements along the way no matter how big or small. When you're having a bad day and things are not going to plan, it's important to reflect and remind yourself how far you've come."

3. "It's also really important to stay pro-active and set yourself goals and also make the most out of any downtime and sometimes you do have to hustle a little to get the ball rolling. Enjoy the ups and downs; it's all part of the exciting journey!"

# THE POWER OF SOCIAL MEDIA

## Essential social media tools and how to make the most of them

There have never been so many tools at our disposal that we can use to promote our business free of charge, and without a significant outlay of time. Social media is one of the most important of these tools.

Once you've decided on your name and bought your domain, it's a good plan to get Facebook, Twitter and Pinterest pages set up that tie in with your brand identity. While you are preparing your launch you can start using these platforms to get your potential customers excited about what you will have to offer. Here are the six key social media platforms to use and, crucially, how best to use them.

### 1. TWITTER

Visit **www.twitter.com**, create an account, start to follow friends and contacts (and their followers) and get tweeting. Follow Mark Shaw's steps for Twitter success.

Cost: free

# 10 steps to Twitter success

*Mark Shaw, author of* Twitter Your Business *and award-winning ex sales guy that advises and trains people how to use Twitter to gain more business and to be effective with their time, provides his ten top tips that will have you using Twitter far more effectively . . .*

1. **Why be on Twitter?** – This is the first question you need to ask yourself. Think about all the possible reasons you may want to utilise Twitter as this will help you to build a useful strategy and give you an indication on possible resources that you will need.

2. **Who will be tweeting?** – Nothing happens on Twitter just by having an account. It needs someone behind it who understands Twitter and enjoys using it. This is not a technical job. The best person to take this role is usually the business owner. They are the ones that are most passionate about their business, fully understand it and can't stop talking about it.

3. **What is success?** Before you start using Twitter it is important that you think about what success would look like for you. You can then put into place ways to measure those things. It may be simply more website traffic, more sales, more sign ups for your newsletter. All these things can be easily measured.

4. **Be committed** – Add a good photo, perhaps a bespoke background, your website URL and an interesting bio. Your bio is only 160 characters so make sure you use all of them. Try and differentiate yourself and make sure it contains keywords so that others can find you.

5. **Be consistent** – Show up each day and tweet even if you don't have much time. It's more important to do a small amount each day than lots on one day and then nothing for a week or so.

6. **Be interesting** – Try and tweet 3 types of messages: social chit-chat; the sharing of resources, links, tools, info, ideas and opinions; and tweets that answer questions which demonstrate your knowledge. Aim for a good balance, that's the key.

7. **Be interested** – Engage with others by answering questions and joining in. Find conversations to enter into via **www.twitter.com/search** and retweet (RT) other people's messages if they are of interest to you and your followers. It's not about selling things but it is all about building your brand and credibility.

8. **Don't automate your Twitter activity.** Twitter is all about being personal and building relationships via conversations. You can't do that if you simply broadcast all day long. Twitter is a communication channel not a broadcast station.

9. **Twitter is a marathon and certainly not a sprint.** You don't need to follow thousands within minutes of joining. Start off slowly, follow a few people, start to see how it works, start to send out a few messages and just observe, listen and learn.

10. **Twitter is a social platform.** So have fun and be sociable. Twitter should not be a chore. It should be something that you enjoy taking part in. Twitter is not a substitute for other marketing activities but a bolt on to other things.

TIP { **The visual touch**

The creative industry loves visuals, so tweeting an image of a design that you are currently working on or a new product is really worthwhile!

## 2. FACEBOOK

Facebook is the most popular social networking site in the world. The site has over 1 billion users worldwide, so if you need to be where your customers are, there's a good chance some of them will be there!

Create a Facebook page (**www.facebook.com/page**) and then share news, photos, and blog posts, anything you think your customers would like to hear about.

You can then advertise to audiences based on location, age and interests. As an advertiser you control how much you want to spend and set a daily budget. The minimum budget is US $1 (63p) a day. After designing your ad(s), decide how long you want the campaign to run and whether you want to be charged for the number of clicks you receive (CPC – charge per click) or the number of times your ad is displayed.

To learn the secrets of succeeding as a business on Facebook, check out the free eBook 'Boost Your Business With Facebook' at: **www.enterprisenation.com/facebook-book-offer**

Listing cost: free

## 3. LINKEDIN

Referring to itself as "the world's largest professional network", LinkedIn has 75 million members in over 200 countries. Visit **www.linkedin.com**, create an account and start connecting with contacts and finding new ones. Form LinkedIn groups around your specialist subject, or, if you are a professional selling creative services, check out the new Creative Portfolio Display application (**linkd.in/deDVX1**), which aims to "empower creative professionals by creating a one-stop solution for maintaining their work portfolio and broadcasting it to millions".

Cost: free (option to upgrade to a business account, which is a paid-for package)

## 4. FLICKR

Join **www.flickr.com** and promote yourself visually by uploading photos of you and your products or service, and maybe even a few shots of happy customers. The site also carries video clips so you can show:

- events you host, speak at, or attend
- products you make as well as images of the production process
- happy customers using/enjoying your products and services
- your workspace
- your family (if you – and they – feel comfortable showing your personal side).

You can also easily pull the photos into your blog and social media pages.

Try to interact with other Flickr users – comment on their photos, add contacts and add your photos to groups.

Cost: free (option to upgrade to a pro account which is a paid-for package)

## 5. YOUTUBE

YouTube is the world's most popular online video community, with 24 hours of video uploaded every minute. Start your own business channel for free, and upload videos profiling you and your work.

Create an account (**www.youtube.com/create_account**), start a channel (advice via YouTube video!), and start broadcasting to the world. You can give each of your videos a name and assign keywords to it to help with searching, plus you can have a short description of your company on your profile page. Again, these clips are very easy to add to your website, and they help keep the content fresh and interesting. Footage can even be filmed for free if you have a webcam in your laptop.

Cost: free

## 6. PINTEREST

Pinterest (**www.pinterest.com**) is a virtual pinboard. You can pin images from anywhere on the internet, and you can also repin pictures from other people's Pinterest pages. It is the third most popular social network site after Facebook and Twitter. Not only is it a great way to gather inspiration and ideas for work, it can also be used as a promotional tool for your business.

The majority of Pinterest users are women and many use it for ideas for their home, making it an essential place to have a presence when starting a creative business.

Here are a few ideas of how you can use Pinterest for business: **www.thesocialmediaguide.com/ social_media/10-creative-ways-pinterest-for-business**

Cost: free

*Total budget required for online promotion: £0*

# MEASURE THE RESULTS

Time to measure what's working and what's not. You'll be pleased to know there's a whole host of tools that are free to use and will show real-time results for what's working on your site and across social media profiles.

Look out, in particular, for the sources of your traffic (which are your highest referring sites) and your most popular pages. You can see days where your site receives spikes in visitor levels (and track this back to marketing) and measure if visitors are spending longer periods on the site and which times are popular, e.g. weekends, evenings, lunchtimes, etc. Google Analytics offers intelligence on your website traffic and marketing effectiveness: **www.google.com/analytics**

There are other analytics options:

- Alexa (**www.alexa.com**) – web traffic metrics, site demographics and top URL listings
- Clicky (**www.clicky.com**) – monitors and analyses your site traffic in real time

- Crazy Egg (**www.crazyegg.com**) – see which pages visitors are visiting, with a colourful heat map

- Opentracker (**www.opentracker.net**) – gather and analyse web stats and monitor online visitors

- StatCounter (**www.statcounter.com**) – an invisible web tracker and hit counter that offers data in real time

- Marketing Grader (**www.websitegrader.com**) – generates a free marketing report that compares your site with a competitor's

If you discover via your analytics review, that a blog or website has featured your business or products, it is good practice to thank them for including you, and also it is worth tweeting the link and/or posting on your Facebook page. The blogger will be pleased you've shared their link, and you will remind your followers that your work is highly regarded in your industry, increasing credibility.

# BEAUTIFUL BUSINESS: GILLIES JONES GLASS

**Name:** Kate Jones & Stephen Gillies

**Business:** Gillies Jones Glass

**Website: www.gilliesjonesglass.co.uk**

**Social media:** @gilliesjones | **www.facebook.com/gilliesjonesglass**

Kate Jones and Stephen Gillies always knew that they wanted to start their own business making handmade glass bowls.

> "Our own studio was always the ambition, and in 1995 we opened our doors in Rosedale, North Yorkshire, after long apprenticeships in the UK, Denmark, Switzerland and the USA."

Kate and Stephen advertised and promoted the new business extensively beforehand, so on the morning the studio opened they got their first customer.

"A priest came to buy a glass decanter for communion wine" Kate remembers, and this was swiftly followed by trade orders from Conran and a design commission from Heals.

From there, the duo have continued to promote the business using a variety of methods, including distributing local leaflets, using local advertising as well as through their website and online social media. Occasionally, Kate and Stephen will also hire PR experts to give the business a boost. They insist on professional photography to show their beautiful products at their best.

Because of this, Gillies Jones Glass has grown steadily, initially working with shops and galleries such as Conran, Liberty, Gumps, Barneys and so on, as well as retailing their work directly from the studio. More recently, they have chosen to concentrate on growing their own customer base and selling smaller pieces directly.

> "We now sell the majority of our limited batch production work ourselves and work with a few specialist galleries for our small bowls, and even fewer galleries with our unique works. We sell online and we sell from our studio, all of which is enabled by new media."

Kate and Stephen work together well, with Stephen blowing the glass, and Kate bringing a well-defined sense of design to the partnership.

"There's just the two of us, and we have some part-time sales help on the weekends so that we spend time with our children and occasionally we bring in a hot shop apprentice."

As such, they are planning to take the business global further down the line. "We hope to expand internationally with our unique works when the children are of an age that allows us more time to travel and develop our work."

Gillies Jones Glass has big plans for 2013, with a new studio exhibition opening in March, as well as another in the summer plus two major gallery exhibitions.

# Top tips!

1. "Work for others first and learn how to run a studio; the making is the easy bit, making a living is harder ..."

2. "The skills required to successfully self-fund your business and make a living are just as important as the skills needed for the physical process. Do not overlook them and do not be afraid to use functional business tools – all the tools can be adapted and used successfully and allow you to keep your integrity – it's what crafting is about."

3. "Selling is not selling out!"

# Chapter Twelve

## HAPPY CUSTOMERS
## & A BALANCED
## BUSINESS

NOW LET'S LOOK at how to keep customers coming back and make sure the business stays in balance as you grow.

# ATTRACT CUSTOMERS BACK

You are making sales and developing a strong community of fans and followers. Give visitors and customers a reason to return by following these steps.

## Fresh and user-generated content

Encourage visitors and customers back to your site with regular posted content, and if it's an e-commerce site, keep the product range updated. Give your site some TLC each day. Fresh content will attract visitors who want to see what's new; it will also appeal to the trawling web spiders who determine search engine results.

Encourage your site visitors to get to know each other through a forum, comment boxes or a plug-in application. Before you know it, a sense of community will develop and visitors will log on each day to find out who's saying what and what's happening.

## Exclusive offers

Extend offers to your existing customers, readers or members that will tempt them back. This offer could be conditional on customers referring a friend: that way your customer returns to the site with others in tow. Add to this with a badge of honour; design an icon that visitors can display on their own site to show their affiliation with you.

## Guest appearances

Invite special guests to appear on your site via guest blog posts, hosting a webchat or a featured interview.

## Keep in touch

Communicate all these good and 'sticky' things to your users through a regular e-newsletter powered by products such as MailChimp (**www.mailchimp.com**) or AWeber Communications (**www.aweber.com**).

TIP { Newsletters people won't delete

Spend time on making your mail-outs look appealing to the recipient. Think about what will make them click through to your website – whether that's images of your new products, a competition, a discount offer or details about the next event you'll be attending or hosting.

Another point to consider is how often to send out your emails. People often unsubscribe from mailing lists if they feel they are receiving too many messages, so make sure your content is interesting, relevant and not too frequent. But be careful that your mail-outs don't become too sporadic and that your customers don't forget about you completely! Perhaps once a week, with an additional promotional email once a fortnight could work? Test it out and see what works best for you.

# KEEP THE BUSINESS IN BALANCE

As the business continues to grow, you will want to maintain momentum and grow at a comfortable pace. Achieve this by following what I call 'the golden triangle', which will keep you and the business in balance. This requires spending roughly a third of your time on three key things:

# 1. Customer care

Look after your customers by delivering a quality product or service, on time and within budget. And remember . . . the customer is always right.

I ask clients for feedback so that I can keep a check on what they're thinking and changes they'd like to see. It's good to know some personal details about your customers, too. (Maybe the date of their birthday, their favourite hobby or names of their children.) As you gather these details, make a quick note so that you can send a birthday card on the right date, enquire after GCSE results at the right time, etc. Don't go overboard, but showing that you care certainly won't harm your relationship.

Offer customers good service, regular communication and an innovative line of products and services. It will stand you in good stead.

# 2. New business

Taking care of customers means taking care of sales. Why? Because it costs less to win business from existing customers than it does to find new ones. And if customers are happy, they'll say good things about you to new and potential customers. This is called word-of-mouth marketing and achieving it is every business owner's dream!

Secure new clients through marketing, encouraging recommendations and direct-sales calls and pitches.

# 3. Admin

Not as enjoyable as the first two, but admin still has to be done. Keep the books in order by raising invoices in good time, being on top of cash flow and filing tax returns and company documents on time and in order. In short, keep the finances in check and the books up-to-date.

# Right on time

Without the old framework of office life, you'll want to keep a grasp on time: planning it, tracking it, and definitely making the most of it. Do so with these on and offline technology solutions.

## FRESHBOOKS

FreshBooks (**www.freshbooks.com**) is an application that tracks the time you spend on projects and turns this into professional-looking invoices. Particularly useful for businesses providing professional and business services.

## REMEMBER THE MILK

Take your task list with you and add to it from anywhere with Remember The Milk (**www.rememberthemilk.com**). This nifty web-based task manager synchs with Google Calendar, Twitter, BlackBerry, iPhone, instant messenger, email and text messages. The basic package is free.

## OTHER TIME TRACKING SOFTWARE

- Cashboard | **www.getcashboard.com**
- Four Four Time | **www.fourfourtime.co.uk**
- TraxTime | **www.spudcity.com/traxtime**

If, like me, you're still a pen-and-paper person, invest in a diary, filofax or wall calendar from stores such as Staples, Rymans or Paperchase.

# Chapter Thirteen

# GROW
## THE BUSINESS
# WITHOUT
## OUTGROWING
## THE HOME

Y̶OUR BUSINESS IS getting known and making money and you're looking at options on how to scale and grow. Achieve this through:

- productising

- going global

- outsourcing.

# PRODUCTISING

If you're creating products or selling design services, you'll have soon realised there are only so many hours available! As scientists haven't yet worked out how to make more of you, in order to grow the business take the knowledge/skill/talent you have and put it in a box.

## Kits

Let's say you're someone making unique dresses for girls.

You can continue to make your signature-style dress by your own hands and at a price to reflect your time and dedication. But you can also add to your product range with a dress kit that comes with all the material and instructions parents need for making their own dress. At the end of the instructions you could include details of where people can upload pictures of their creations to your blog or website, creating a sense of community and expanding the reach of your brand.

Now you can sell more products (admittedly at a lower price) at the same time as your old successful line.

This is what *Country Living* Magazine's Kitchen Table Talent Award winner, Katherine Prentice (**www.katherineprenticedesigns.co.uk**), is now considering.

> "I'm developing kits as I can make these in higher volumes and at a fraction of the cost of my handbooks, notebooks and purses. The good thing is the kits will work to promote my brand,

generate revenue and ensure my products reach a wider number of people. For me, it feels the right way to grow."

## Courses

Maybe you're selling works of art or designing kitchens and want to 'productise'. Kits are out – but how about launching and teaching a series of classes? You get to meet customers and have your name and brand appear in front of more people. You can even sell your produce at the classes! They'll also provide excellent photo opportunities for local press.

When it comes to looking for space for such a class, consider your own home or approach the owner of the local coffee shop to ask if they would be happy for you to use the space at times when they are usually quiet; that way you're likely to get space for free in return for introducing footfall. Other places to consider could be your library, community centre, church hall or even a local business.

Similarly if you are selling online, you could think about occasionally holding a pop-up or customer event. This gives local customers and press the chance to come and meet you and view your products in person which is a great way to connect with your customer base and network with press contacts.

When in the business of providing business services, the options for publishing may be the best route for you to follow to sell your knowledge to a wider audience, i.e. publishing a book, producing a podcast, and charging people for access this content.

# GOING GLOBAL

There's never been a better time to look beyond domestic shores for business. By virtue of having a professional window to the world (i.e. a website!), start-ups and small businesses are going global faster than ever before.

In my book, *Go Global: How to take your business to the world*, I show how you can increase trade and broaden horizons in five simple steps. You will also find a free *Go Global* eBook on Enterprise Nation and a downloadable app – all the tools you need to be running an internationally successful business!

# OUTSOURCING

Grow profits by focusing on what you do best and outsourcing the rest. It's perfectly possible to achieve this and manage an expanding team from your own small or home office.

What can be outsourced, and to whom?

## ADMIN

Hire a VA (virtual assistant) to do the admin tasks you don't want or don't have the time to do. Visit VA directories and resources to find your perfect match.

- International Association of Virtual Assistants | **www.iava.org.uk**
- Society of Virtual Assistants | **www.societyofvirtualassistants.co.uk**
- Time Etc | **www.timeetc.co.uk**
- VA Success Group | **www.vasuccessgroup.co.uk**
- The Virtual Assistant Coaching & Training Company Co. | **www.vact.co.uk**

## PR, MARKETING AND DESIGN

Outsource your PR to a specialist who can be pitching and promoting the business whilst you're at work. Find skilled professionals on directory sites such as Enterprise Nation and Business Smiths or contact companies such as PrPro, Press for Attention PR and Just In Time PR.

- Enterprise Nation | **www.enterprisenation.com**
- Business Smiths | **www.businesssmiths.co.uk**
- PrPro | **www.prpro.co.uk**
- Press for Attention PR | **www.pressforattention.com**
- Just In Time PR | **www.justintimepr.com**

## SALES

Hire a sales expert to make calls, set up appointments and attend trade shows. Find these professionals on Enterprise Nation (**www.enterprisenation.com**), contact telemarketing companies that offer outbound sales calls as a service, or look at sales specialists such as Inside and professionals like Jackie Wade.

- Great Guns | **www.greatgunsmarketing.co.uk**
- Inside | **www.theinsideteam.co.uk**
- Winning Sales | **www.winningsales.co.uk**

## CUSTOMER SERVICE

Looking after your customers is vital, but even that can be outsourced to great effect. Get Satisfaction's (**www.getsatisfaction.com**) tagline is "people-powered customer service" – it provides a web-hosted platform, much like a forum, where customers can ask questions, suggest improvements, report a problem or give praise. It can save you time and money by making customer service an open process that leverages the wisdom of crowds. Questions are answered by other users, rather than you as the site host.

You don't want to outsource this completely as it's good to show personal contact with customers, but this is a useful tool that could improve your business as customers offer their feedback.

## ACCOUNTS

Unless you are in the accountancy business, your accounts are almost a must to be outsourced.

Monthly payroll, accounts, VAT returns and corporate tax returns all take time and it's time you can't afford or simply don't have. A cost/benefit analysis is likely to show that it's cheaper to outsource to a qualified accountant.

Ask around for recommendations of accountants in your area who deliver a quality service at a competitive cost and are registered with the Institute of Chartered Accountants in England and Wales.

For online accounting and invoicing that makes life easier for you and your accountant, check out:

- FreeAgent  |  **www.freeagent.com**
- KashFlow  |  **www.kashflow.co.uk**
- Liquid Accounts  |  **www.liquidaccounts.net**
- QuickBooks  |  **www.quickbooks.co.uk**
- Sage One  |  **www.sageone.com/accounts**

# Steps to successful outsourcing

## DO THE GROUNDWORK

Spend some time working on the task yourself so that you've built some foundations before handing it over to a third party. For example, if you outsource sales then have a ready-made contacts list and some open doors that the specialist can build on, rather than starting from scratch. This will make it more cost-effective for you and means they hit the ground running.

## BE CLEAR ON THE BRIEF

Having spent some time doing the task yourself, you will have a clear idea of the brief. Back to the example of outsourcing sales, if you've spent six to 12 months sourcing leads and making contacts, you'll have a much clearer idea of the type of prospecting the specialist should do. The clearer the brief, the better the results.

## TAKE YOUR TIME

Take your time and take references. Spend time evaluating the specialists in the market and, if you can, talk to their existing clients. Do they have the industry experience you're after? Will they represent your brand in a professional manner? Have they shown commitment to other clients? When an outsourced arrangement works well, the partner becomes part of your team so choose them as carefully as you would choose an employee.

## LET GO!

Outsourcing a key function means having to let go a little. Someone else becomes accountable for these results. Embrace this rather than resist it. As the business owner you remain in ultimate control but the expert will need their own space in which to flourish. Outsourcing can save you time and help make you money. Finding the right partner, on the right terms, will make you feel like a new and liberated person.

# Form teams

Once you've chosen your outsourced partners, it's important to keep in regular contact and work together as a team. There are a number of online project management and collaboration tools to help you stay on top of projects and in control of the company.

- Basecamp (**www.basecamp.com**) is the project management tool we rely on at Enterprise Nation. This is a top-class product that allows you to create projects, invite people to view them, upload files and make comments. It's effective online project management that can be accessed from anywhere.

- Share documents via Google with Google Docs (**docs.google.com**). You can edit on the move, choose who accesses documents and share changes in real-time.

- Huddle (**www.huddle.com**) offers simple and secure online workspaces. Huddle is hosted, so there's no software to download and it's free to get started.

- Work with anyone, anywhere with GoToMeeting (**www.gotomeeting.com**), an easy-to-use online meeting tool.

- Share and record meeting notes with Ketchup (**www.useketchup.com**).

- Pow Wow Now (**www.powwownow.co.uk**) offers conference calling at 'open access' level. Priced packages available.

- Skype (**www.skype.com/allfeatures/conferencecall**) allows free and easy-to-use conference calls.

TIP { Help from an entern

Consider hiring an entern (**www.enternships.com**). Enterns are enthusiastic students and graduates, passionate about entrepreneurship and looking for work experience in young start-up companies.

# Form partnerships

If relationships with other companies and self-employed professionals develop you may decide to form a partnership. Consider writing a partnership agreement as your 'pre-nup' in business. At the outset of a relationship, all is good and you're excited about the potential, but it's best to be safe; have a few things written and agreed so all parties are clear on expectations.

The following should not be taken as concrete legal advice, more of a guideline on how to draw up an agreement. An agreement need only be a single page and cover the basics:

## SCOPE OF AGREEMENT

What is your partnership working to achieve? For example, "This agreement is made between Company A and Company B. The agreement is related to the generation of online advertising revenues/hosting of an event/development of a new product."

## RESPECTIVE RESPONSIBILITIES

Set out the expectations on who does what. For example, Company A will be responsible for promotion and business development and Company B will take on technical development and client care. Also include a note of how you'll keep each other briefed, maybe through the use of an online project management tool such as Basecamp.

## FINANCES

What will be the split in revenue, and is this before or after costs? And who owns the intellectual property of the product/service/activity? Consider including a clause that states the agreement will be reviewed in six months so that both parties can check on progress and have the right to terminate the agreement if it hasn't gone as planned.

## BE FAIR

Agreements where both parties feel they're receiving their fair share are likely to be longer-lasting than those when one party feels embittered. Talk about this before writing and concluding the agreement. Make sure there's no resentment or sense of being exploited on either side.

## SIGN IT!

After making the effort to produce an agreement, be sure to both sign it! And then store it so you can access it easily if the need arises.

When writing the clauses in your agreement, think about all the things that could go wrong and safeguard against them. It's a practical exercise and won't harm your newly formed business relationship but will get it off on a firm footing. If you're looking for a template agreement, check out the following sites:

- Clickdocs | **www.clickdocs.co.uk**
- Off to see my lawyer | **www.offtoseemylawyer.com**

# BEAUTIFUL BUSINESS:
# PATCHWORK HARMONY & *91 MAGAZINE*

**Name:** Caroline Taylor

**Business:** Patchwork Harmony & *91 Magazine*

**Website:** www.patchworkharmony.co.uk | www.91magazine.co.uk

**Social media:** www.facebook.com/patchworkharmony | @patchworkhrmy | @91magazine

Caroline Taylor's journey into the world of small business started back in 2008.

> "I had only been in full-time employment for three years and already I was feeling my creativity was becoming stifled despite working in the photographic industry in which I'd trained. My interest in interiors and vintage style was growing as I set up home with my boyfriend, and I decided I needed a creative hobby to fulfil what I felt was missing in my day job."

A friend suggested blogging, and Caroline fell in love with it and the world that surrounds it!

> "I found it so inspiring to engage with other people who had shared interests. It wasn't long after that, in early 2009, that I opened my online boutique selling vintage homewares."

The idea for Patchwork Harmony came purely from being inspired by all the lovely things she was finding online through blogging. Caroline realised that it was something she could start from home without giving up her day job.

Patchwork Harmony's first customer came with the launch of the shop, as she was commissioned to write a feature about design blogging for the newspaper she worked for as a picture editor.

> "Being an international publication the coverage reached out across the world and my first customer was actually outside the UK!"

This initial brush with the effects of press coverage made Caroline realise the importance of gaining good editorial placement. She set about contacting as many journalists as she could find in interiors magazines and newspapers. In the first year she received quite a lot of publicity.

"I also listed my website on directories that were specific to my industry and continued to blog and network within the niche community."

In order to grow the business further, Caroline joined Not On The High Street (**www.notonthehighstreet.com**) and listed some of her items on other partner sites.

"I paid to feature one of my products in the Not On The High Street Christmas catalogue for two years running which gave a huge boost to sales around an important time of the year."

In 2011, Caroline had the idea to combine her experience in publishing with everything she'd learnt through blogging and running her shop. She would start up an online magazine.

"The plan was that the magazine would feature similar topics I was covering on my blog, such as thrifty ways to style your home, craft ideas and interviews with creative entrepreneurs. And in October 2011 the first issue of *91 Magazine* launched!"

Since then, she has made the decision to refocus her energies mainly on the magazine, blog and other editorial work. She has downsized her shop significantly. As part of this, Caroline has brought in a new deputy editor and a researcher, who helps her put the magazine together.

"I also work with a wide range of contributors from writers, bloggers, photographers, stylists and illustrators. I've found that I much prefer working with people than by myself, as it's much more motivating."

Both Patchwork Harmony and *91 Magazine* have been international from day one.

"Both are online ventures so they are already open to the global market, which is the undeniable advantage of internet business. Your customer base is not confined to one postcode!"

Caroline has had orders from all corners of the world and the readership of *91 Magazine* is also international.

"This is mainly down to bloggers from around the world featuring what I do – I have seen posts about *91 Magazine* in French, Polish and Turkish to name a few. The love of beautiful things is definitely a global one!"

In December 2012, *91 Magazine* also won a Women In Publishing New Venture award which recognises Caroline's achievements since she started the business.

"*91 Magazine* has been my little baby for the last year and a half, and it was so wonderful to be awarded this from such a great organisation that has been running since 1979. It was also such a lovely way to finish off 2012 and really our first year of *91 Magazine*."

Patchwork Harmony has evolved greatly since it began in 2008 and Caroline plans to use the next twelve months to continue this process.

"I am excited to get more creative and produce original and engaging content – I plan to expand my client list for the creative services branch of the business and I am also offering one-to-one creative business advice to start-ups. The plan is to start promoting these aspects of what I do more widely."

# Top tips!

1. "Do your research at the start. Immerse yourself in your industry, find out what it is people want and consider if what you have to offer really fits in with the market."

2. "Network online and offline – it is a saturated market so you must make yourself stand out from the crowd, and it really helps to make contacts."

3. "Do not underestimate the power of social media! Fellow small business owners are a friendly, helpful bunch who often share knowledge and expertise, so learn from others where possible."

4. "Don't scrimp on the important things – whether you are online or not, good photography of your products is essential as this helps to gain press coverage both in magazines and in the blog world. Save on other areas; for example, shop around for good offers on packaging. eBay is a great resource for this."

5. "Finally, be aware that running a small business is not a career choice; it is a lifestyle choice. Whether you start up while still holding down other employment or if you decide to give that up to pursue your dream, remember that it is all-consuming. You will have sleepless nights worrying, fretting or perhaps, like me, coming up with your most ingenious ideas at 3am! But it really is the most rewarding thing you can ever do. Receiving positive feedback from customers, clients or your peers is so much more satisfying and life-affirming than that big bonus paycheck in a corporate job!"

# HELP AND SUPPORT

As a tweet to me once said "asking for help does not make you weak, but it could make you a success". Ask questions at every opportunity; of your peers, of mentors and accredited business advisors. Here's where to find them.

## Peers

Who better to turn to than those who are also going through the experience of starting and growing a business? Visit the following sites and join their active forums and communities of business owners who will be more than happy to help.

• BusinessZone | **www.businesszone.co.uk**

• Start Up Donut | **www.startupdonut.co.uk**

• *Business Matters* magazine | **www.bmmagazine.co.uk**

• Enterprise Nation | **www.enterprisenation.com**

## Mentors

The coalition government has announced a national mentoring programme and the recruitment of no fewer than 40,000 mentors who will be on hand to help young and start-up businesses. Details on how to find a mentor are still to come, but keep your eyes on the Department for Business, Innovation & Skills (BIS) at **www.bis.gov.uk**. A useful site on mentoring can also be found at: **www.mentorsme.co.uk**

### THOUGHTS ON A MENTOR

Over the ten-years-plus of running my own business, I have developed a view on mentors. It may not be a view with which you agree, as each business owner is different. But this is what has worked for me.

Don't restrict yourself to one mentor! I have learnt from many people as my businesses have passed through different stages of development. I would approach the person I felt best placed to have the answer, take on board their views, consider my options, and then act.

The ideal mentor is someone who possesses four things:

1. experience of your industry/sector

2. the ability to listen

3. the technical skills to advise

4. a willingness to make introductions to useful contacts.

If you can find these in one person, you are a fortunate person.

One of the finest things a mentor can do is allow you to talk. By doing so, you will often find you work out the answer. You sometimes just need a sounding board to answer your own question.

## ACCREDITED ADVISORS

When starting and growing your business, consider approaching your local enterprise agency for support. The National Enterprise Network acts as an umbrella organisation for all agencies so you can find your local contact at **www.nationalenterprisenetwork.org**. Local business advisors can help with everything from business planning to applying for funds and financial forecasting.

## PRIVATE ONE-TO-ONE ADVICE / NICHE ONLINE COURSES

Similar to mentors, experienced small business owners can advise on your new business and share their personal experiences and tricks of the trade.

You can also sign up for small focused course such as Holly Becker's 'Blog your own way' e-course which focuses specifically on creative blogging, completed from the comfort of your own home: **www.decor8blog.com/ecourses**

Caroline Taylor of Patchwork Harmony also offers private one-to-one advice sessions suited to your own personal requirements: **www.patchworkharmony.co.uk/index.php/creative-services**

# StartUp Britain

In March 2011, the StartUp Britain (**www.startupbritain.co**) campaign was launched to encourage more people to start a business and support existing businesses to grow. The campaign is run by a team of eight business owners and entrepreneurs, with support from the government and a number of corporate sponsors.

The face of the campaign is a website which offers links to useful resources and content, as well as valuable offers from large corporates and leading brands. Visit the site to be inspired and to celebrate the start-ups of Britain.

# Enterprise Nation

Turn to Enterprise Nation as your central resource and friend in business. Every month we:

- profile small business success stories
- release eBooks on topics that matter most
- produce videos with bite-sized business advice
- host webchats with experts and special guests
- develop new tools to help you increase sales and reduce costs
- connect you to peers via the Directory and social media.

Enterprise Nation is the place where you can access advice and support, raise profile and make sales.

- **www.enterprisenation.com**
- @e_nation

# CONCLUSION

I hope you've enjoyed this book about turning your passion for interiors into a business and becoming your own boss.

It should have shown you that there has never been a better time to set up on your own. You can begin in a small way, using your evenings and weekends to develop your skills and test the market. A huge amount of support is available to you from enterprise agencies and business support groups, as well as from peers and mentors.

Focus on your idea, work on your sales and marketing, take care of your customers, watch over your cash flow and you will soon have a business of which you can be proud!

I wish you every success on your exciting business journey.

Emma Jones

# GET THE BEST
# SUPPORT
## FOR YOUR
# SMALL BUSINESS

### JOIN ENTERPRISE NATION: A thoroughly modern business club

* Free business eBooks
* Discounts on business events
* Exclusive business benefits – including access to over 1,000 workspaces in 85 countries

**Enterprise Nation helps thousands of people turn their good ideas into great businesses.**

We also represent your views in the heart of government.

So, take your business to the next level – with comprehensive support, including marketing help, networking opportunities and over £500-worth of exclusive business benefits.

**Join the club now for just £20 per year – and get a FREE Enterprise Nation mug!**

## Find out more at www.enterprisenation.com